The Prevention of Nuclear War

A United Nations Perspective

William Epstein

Special Fellow,
United Nations Institute for Training and Research

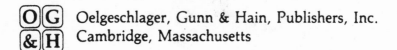

Oelgeschlager, Gunn & Hain, Publishers, Inc.
Cambridge, Massachusetts

THE PREVENTION OF NUCLEAR WAR

International Standard Book Number: 0-89946-184.

Library of Congress Catalog Card Number:

Printed in the U.S.A.

Library of Copngress Cataloging in Publication Data

Epstein, William,
  The prevention of nuclear war.

  Includes bibliographical references and index:
  1. Atomic weapons and disarmament. I. Title.
JX1974.7.E556 1984   327.1'74   84-2248
ISBN 0-89946-184-0
U.N. sales number E.84.XV.RR/30

Contents

v

vi

Foreword

This book is one of three studies the United Nations Institute for Training and Research (UNITAR) is devoting to the prevention of nuclear war. The project under which the three studies were launched was initiated in 1982 in response to recommendations by the United Nations General Assembly that UNITAR focus greater attention on studies dealing with international peace and security, disarmament and the prevention of nuclear war.

It was decided that three manuscripts be produced: one from a United Nations perspective, one from a United States perspective, and one to reflect the viewpoint of Soviet scientists. The last has already been published. The three studies constitute a trilogy that is intended to provide comprehensive coverage of the problem of preventing nuclear war.

The research project in its entirety was envisaged as a means for analyzing a subject of fundamental interest to the cause of world peace, the threat of a nuclear war and of possible ways to avert it. It deals with the issues related to the development, production, deployment and use of nuclear weapons, and with the measures proposed for preventing the proliferation of these weapons by the nuclear and non-nuclear powers and for halting and reversing the nuclear arms race.

The world today is faced with an escalating arms race and the threat of possible nuclear war. Intensive new efforts are necessary to remove the threat of war, to preserve international security and to impart insight into the positions of all the primary actors who influence our security. This volume has been prepared by a specialist in the field of disarmament who was for a number of years the senior official in charge of disarmament in the United Nations Secretariat. It reflects the United Nations perspective and, together with the other two, will constitute an important contribution to the understanding of questions that are basic to human survival.

The views and conclusions in this study are the responsibility of the author and do not necessarily reflect the opinions of UNITAR or of its Board of Trustees. Although UNITAR takes no position on the views and conclusions expressed by the authors of its studies, it does assume responsibility for determining whether a study merits publication.

Michel Doo Kingue
Executive Director

Preface

This study has resulted from over a third of a century of my own direct involvement in the international efforts for disarmament. I served as a member of the United Nations Secretariat in charge of disarmament, as a representative of the Secretary-General at many of the negotiations, and as a member of the Canadian Delegation to six sessions of the General Assembly.

During that time I have seen hopes for disarmament and averting the threat of nuclear war rise and fall. They invariably have risen and progress has been made towards disarmament during periods of relaxation of tension; likewise they invariably have fallen and deadlock has ensued during periods of tension. I have thus come to the not very original or surprising conclusion that the chances for disarmament and avoiding the risks of a nuclear war depend on the state of relations between the two major nuclear powers, the Union of Soviet Socialist Republics and the United States of America. Agreement on arms control measures tend to reflect the state of political relations between these two powers, but they also tend to have a positive influence on those relations.

I have also come to the same conclusion that was emphasized in the Final Document of the first Special Session on Disarmament, namely, that while it is possible to halt, freeze, or set a limit to the nuclear arms race—important and difficult tasks—without significant progress towards improving national and international security, it is probably not possible, indeed it is highly unlikely, that far-reaching measures of disarmament can be achieved without parallel progress in improving or strengthening international security. This, of course, requires that all nations, and in particular the nuclear powers and other militarily significant states, should feel more secure. While international security must be established on a global basis, in large part it, too, depends on the state of relations between the two major powers.

This study is intended to reflect the United Nations point of view. The selection of topics, the arrangement of subject matter, and the interpretation and assessment of the United Nation's actions are, of course, my own.

I have attempted to survey, in chapter 2, all the past activities of the world organization relevant to the prevention of nuclear war, and, in chapter 3, some recent, important developments on the international scene. In chapter 4, I have set forth my personal observations and conclusions.

I must express my great appreciation to my friends, namely, Alessandro Corradini, consultant to the Department for Disarmament Affairs, Mohamed El-Baradei of the United Nations Institute for Training and Research, and Paul Szasz of the Office of Legal Affairs, for their kindness in reading the manuscript and in making many valuable suggestions for improving it. They are not responsible, of course, for any of the opinions or assessments set forth.

Chapter 1

Introduction

The United Nations was established to "save succeeding genera-
tions from the scourage of war." Indeed, the United Nations itself is
envisaged as the instrument and means for preventing wars and international armed conflicts of every nature and kind.

Article 1, paragraph 1, of the Charter of the United Nations specifies
that the first purpose of the United Nations is the maintenance of international peace and security, and that the primary means to that end
is the taking of "effective collective measures" to prevent and remove
threats to peace and to suppress acts of aggression or other breaches
of peace. To achieve that purpose, all Member States are bound to settle their international disputes by peaceful means and to refrain from
the threat or use of force.

The Charter makes no reference to nuclear weapons because it was
signed on 26 June 1945, six weeks before the explosion of the Hiroshima
bomb and some three weeks before the first nuclear test explosion. The
Charter not only makes no reference to nuclear weapons, but it makes
very little reference to either disarmament or the regulation of armaments. Indeed, Articles 1 and 2 of the Charter, setting forth the purposes and principles of the Organization, contain not a single reference
to disarmament. Article 11 includes the "principles governing disar-

5

mament and the regulation of armaments" among "the general principles of co-operation in the maintenance of international peace and security," concerning which the General Assembly can make recommendations to the members or to the Security Council. Article 26 is more specific: "In order to promote the establishment and maintenance of international peace and security with the least diversion for armaments of the world's human and economic resources, the Security Council shall be responsible for formulating, with the assistance of the Military Staff Committee referred to in Article 47, plans to be submitted to the Members of the United Nations for the establishment of a system for the regulation of armaments." Article 47, which creates and defines the responsibilities of the Military Staff Committee, gives it the task, among others: "to advise and assist the Security Council on all questions relating to . . . the regulation of armaments, and possible disarmament."

One of the reasons for the relatively little attention devoted to arms control and disarmament in the United Nations Charter is that the system of peacekeeping and enforcement measures envisaged by Chapter VII of the Charter was predicated upon the continued existence of national armies, navies, and air forces. These were to be made available to the Security Council to maintain or restore international peace and security, and were to be used only for self-defense in the case of an armed attack against a member of the United Nations, until the Security Council could take the necessary measures.

Nevertheless, the Charter has been fully adequate to deal with all aspects of the problem of disarmament, including nuclear weapons. Those who wished to ensure that nuclear energy would be used for peace and not for war saw the United Nations as the obvious and natural agency to achieve that goal.

From the beginning of the work of the world community, it was recognized that disarmament, together with the peaceful settlement of disputes and enforcement measures in case of a breach of peace, were three pillars of the United Nations system for preserving international peace and security. Unfortunately, in the earliest years of the United Nations, the Cold War and the breakdown in East-West relations made it impossible to implement Article 43 and the enforcement provisions of the Charter. These provide for placing national armed forces at the disposal of the Security Council in order to maintain international peace and security. The basic conflict of views between the Soviet Union and the United States continues so that at present and for the foreseeable future there does not appear to be any likelihood of being able to establish this so-called international police force to maintain peace. Instead other efforts must be made to preserve peace: collective measures, including disarmament as well as the peaceful settlement of disputes, and the continued development of the practice of creating *ad hoc* peacekeeping forces that would, with the consent of the parties to a conflict, act as a buffer force rather than as a coercive enforcement force to help preserve the peace.

Progress in disarmament was halted by the Cold War. Many proposals and plans were put forward for ending the arms race in both nuclear and conventional weapons, but to no avail. The first resolution adopted by the United Nations[1] was on the "Establishment of a Commission to Deal with the Problems Raised by the Discovery of Atomic Energy;" it created the Atomic Energy Commission to make proposals to ensure the use of atomic energy for peaceful purposes only and for the elimination of atomic weapons and all other weapons of mass distruction. Despite several years of intensive efforts, no real progress was made. The years of deadlock seemed to have ended by 1961, however, when the United States and the Soviet Union agreed on a "Joint Statement of Agreed Principles for Disarmament Negotiations,"[2] which was approved by the General Assembly in resolution 1722 (XVI) on 20 December 1961, as the basis for the work of a newly-created, Eighteen-Nation Disarmament Committee whose task was to reach agreement on general and complete disarmament under effective international control. In March and April 1962, the United States and the Soviet Union each submitted to the Eighteen-Nation Committee on Disarmament draft outlines for a treaty on general and complete disarmament; but because of fundamental differences between the two sides on not only the measures and stages of disarmament, but also on the questions of balance, control, and the creation of a peacekeeping force to maintain international security, the negotiations quickly reached an impasse.

During the years of deadlock, the two main parties were so far apart in their basic approaches that none of their proposals or plans had any real chance of success. In retrospect, it seems clear that the respective proposals would not be and, indeed, perhaps were not intended to be, acceptable to the other side.

As relations between East and West began to warm up, and as the Cold War began to thaw, the United States and the Soviet Union began to agree on specific arms limitation measures. The easing of tension and the development of detente became both the symptom and the cause of the process. In the two decades from 1959 to 1979, the Soviet Union and the United States entered into a number of multilateral treaties and bilateral agreements. The most important of them are:

Multilateral Treaties

1. The Antartic Treaty (1959)
2. Treaty Banning Nuclear Weapon Tests in the Atmosphere, in Outer Space and Under Water (1963), known as the "Partial Test Ban Treaty"
3. Treaty on the Principles Governing the Activities of States in the Exploration and Use or Outer Space, including the Moon and other Celestial Bodies (1967), known as the "Outer Space Treaty"
4. Treaty for the Prohibition of Nuclear Weapons in Latin America (1967), known as the "Treaty of Tlatelolco"
5. Treaty on the Non-Proliferation of Nuclear Weapons (1968), known as the "Non-Proliferation Treaty"
6. Treaty on the Prohibition of the Emplacement of Nuclear Weapons and other Weapons of Mass Destruction on the Seabed and the Ocean Floor and in the Subsoil Thereof (1971), known as the "Seabed Treaty"
7. Convention on the Prohibition of the Development, Production and Stockpiling of Bacteriological (Biological) and Toxic Weapons and on their Destruction (1972), known as the "Biological Weapons Convention" or "BW Convention"
8. Convention on the Prohibition of Military or Any Other Hostile Use of Environmental Modification Techniques (1977), known as the "ENMOD Convention"
9. Convention on Prohibitions and Restrictions on the Use of Certain Conventional Weapons Which May be Deemed to be Excessively Injurious or to have Indiscriminate Effects (1980), known as the "Inhumane Weapons Convention"

Bilateral Soviet-American Treaties and Agreements

1. Memorandum regarding the Establishment of a Direct Communications Link (1963), known as the "Hotline Agreement"
2. Agreement on Measures to Reduce the Risk of the Outbreak of Nuclear War between the United States and the Soviet Union (1971), known as the "Nuclear Accidents Agreement"
3. Agreement on Measures to Improve the U. S. A.-USSR Direct Communications Link (1971), known as the "Hotline Improvement Agreement"
4. Treaty on the Limitation of Anti-ballistic Missile Systems (1972), known as the "ABM Treaty"
5. Interim Agreement on Certain Measures with Respect to the

Limitation of Strategic Offensive Arms (1972), known as the "SALT I Interim Agreement"

6. Agreement on the Prevention of Incidents On and Over the High Seas" (1972), known as the "Incidents at Sea Agreement"
7. Agreement on the Prevention of Nuclear War (1973)
8. Protocol to the Treaty on the Limitation of Anti-ballistic Missile Systems (1974), known as the "ABM Protocol"
9. Treaty on the Limitation of Underground Nuclear Weapon Tests (1974), known as the "Threshold Test Ban Treaty"*
10. Treaty on Underground Nuclear Explosions for Peaceful Purposes (1976), known as the "Peaceful Nuclear Explosions Treaty*
11. Treaty on the Limitation of Strategic Offensive Arms, and Protocol to the Treaty (1979), known as the "SALT II Treaty*
12. Memorandum regarding the Establishment of a Data Base (1979), known as the "Agreed Data Base"
13. Joint Statement of Principles and Basic Guidelines for Subsequent Negotiations on the Limitation of Strategic Arms (1979), known as the "SALT II Joint Statement of Principles"

The achievement of this impressive list of twenty-two treaties and agreements, however, has not served to halt or reverse the arms race in either nuclear or conventional weaponry. Indeed, it has not even succeeded by any measurable test in slowing it down. The arms race in both categories of weapons is proceeding at a faster pace than ever before in peacetime, with new types of more accurate and lethal weapons of mass destruction, and modernized versions of older weapons, being continually tested, produced and deployed. Since 1959, military global expenditures have grown sixfold and have now reached the astronomical sum of more than 700 billion dollars a year. And no end is in sight.

The continued accumulation and proliferation of more and more weapons multiplies the danger of war in general and of nuclear war in particular. Since the founding of the United Nations, there have been more than one hundred armed conflicts in the world, with tens of millions dead. Fears that a local or regional war fought with conventional weapons could escalate to a nuclear war and threaten the very survival of mankind have alarmed the peoples and nations of the world. In 1978, at the first Special Session of the United Nations General Assembly devoted to disarmament the Assembly declared:[3]

Mankind today is confronted with an unprecedented threat of self-extinction arising from the massive and competitive accumulation of the

---

* Has not been ratified or entered into force

most destructive weapons ever produced. Existing arsenals of nuclear weapons alone are more than sufficient to destroy all life on earth. Failure of efforts to halt and reverse the arms race, in particular the nuclear arms race, increases the danger of the proliferation of nuclear weapons. Yet the arms race continues. Military budgets are constantly growing, with enormous consumption of human and material resources. The increase in weapons, especially nuclear weapons, far from helping to strengthen international security, on the contrary weakens it. The vast stockpiles and tremendous build-up of arms and armed forces and the competition for qualitative refinement of weapons of all kinds to which scientific resources and technological advances are diverted, pose incalculable threats to peace . . .

Removing the threat of a world war—a nuclear war—is the most acute and urgent task of the present day. Mankind is confronted with a choice: we must halt the arms race and proceed to disarmament or face annihilation.

This study will outline the past efforts of the United Nations to grapple with the problem of preventing nuclear war, describe some important elements of the current situation in that regard, and attempt to assess the future needs and possibilities for achieving that goal.

In surveying the historical record, the study reviews all the relevant treaties and agreements that have been achieved and that are binding in international law, as well as the many recommendations of the General Assembly that express the will of the community of nations but are not considered binding. Within each category, some are of greater importance than others and an attempt has been made to assess their relative significance.

While it is evident that drastic reductions in the number of nuclear weapons and their eventual elimination would be the best guarantee for the prevention of nuclear war, this is, even if feasible, a very long-term process. Some countries have therefore concentrated on the prohibition of the use of nuclear weapons, or renunciation of their first use, as the most promising, immediate step towards preventing nuclear war, while pursuing the longer term goal of nuclear disarmament. Others have maintained that the outbreak of nuclear war as a result of accident, miscalculation, uncertainty or panic is a greater danger than a nuclear war occurring as a result of deliberate design or intention, and have therefore stressed the importance of measures to reduce the risk of such accidental nuclear war.

All three approaches are valid, but more progress has been made with respect to the third one, measures to reduce the risk of accidental or unintended nuclear war, than on either nuclear disarmament or on renouncing or banning or even limiting the use of nuclear weapons. It is, of course, much easier to agree on administrative or consultative arrangements for limiting or reducing risks than for limiting or reducing the weapons themselves or restricting their use. In fact, it has been noted that restrictions on the use of nuclear weapons will also reduce the risk of accidental as well as of intentional nuclear war, but this is a substantive measure of such importance that it is usually considered as a separate category and not as a procedural or administrative arrangement to reduce the risks of accidental nuclear war.

~ The main reason for the failure to make greater progress towards nuclear and general disarmament is the basic and continuing fear and mistrust between the two main powers, the United States and the Soviet Union, who are often referred to by others, but not by themselves, as "the super powers."

~ This fear and mistrust results from a complex of factors including the differences between the political, economic and social structures of the two societies, their different approaches and values, and their worldwide competition for power and influence. Each perceives the other as having hostile intentions and as seeking world domination.

~ The United States and its allies consider that the Soviet Union has marked superiority in conventional arms and forces, particularly in Europe, and that they must rely on nuclear weapons to deter any conventional attack. In addition to their conviction that nuclear deterrence continues to be the most effective safeguard against aggression and war, they also consider that they would have great difficulty in obtaining approval by their legislatures for the even larger military expenditures that would be required for the massive conventional arms and forces that would be sufficient to counter those of the Soviet Union without the threat to use nuclear weapons. The Soviet Union considers that it has had to strive mightily to catch up with the United States and to achieve parity in nuclear weaponry. At present, each power accuses the other of seeking nuclear superiority.

~ The United States regards its society as free and open and that of the Soviet Union as authoritarian and closed. It insists on effective international verification because, without it, the open societies might be the only ones bound to comply with arms control agreements. The Soviet Union resists international inspection and verification which it fears may be used for extraneous purposes, such as acquiring intelligence or attempting to undermine its system. It claims that the United States wants verification and control without disarmament.

The United States' freedom to negotiate and to ratify arms control treaties is subject to diverse pressures and frequent changes in its political climate and processes, which can lead to frustration in long term negotiations. This, too, is a factor that makes it easier to negotiate the less complicated agreements to reduce the risk of war than to reduce the weapons of war.

Agreements to reduce the risk of war do in fact help to reduce the risk of a nuclear war, whether by design or intention or, as is more likely, by accident, miscalculation, failure of communications, escalation of a conventional or regional war, or by some other unintended way. Both powers seem to understand the continuing threat posed by nuclear weapons and to have a real desire to limit or reduce the threat, but the agreements achieved are nowhere near sufficient by themselves to eliminate the danger of nuclear war. A majority of states, in particular the non-aligned and like-minded countries, have repeatedly asserted their views that the two powers are more interested in managing the arms race than in ending it.

Nevertheless, despite the formidable obstacles and the intractability of the problem, the United Nations continues to persevere in its efforts to make progress towards the goal of general and complete disarmament, beginning with the cessation of the nuclear arms race and nuclear disarmament, which it regards as the best way to ensure that there will be no nuclear war.

The term "disarmament" is used in this study, in accordance with the customary practice of the United Nations, as a generic term covering all measures relating to the field, including small steps to build confidence, or for arms limitation and control, as well as larger steps for the regulation, reduction or elimination of armaments, armed forces and military expenditures.

After going through several types of committees that dealt with disarmament, such as the Atomic Energy Commission and the Commission for Conventional Armaments, the United Nations has settled on the First Committee of the General Assembly and on the Disarmament Commission, which comprise all the members of the Organization (158 at present), as the deliberative bodies, and on the Committee of Disarmament (now called the Conference on Disarmament), which at present comprises 40 members and meets in Geneva, as the main negotiation forum. The Security Council retains all of the powers vested in it by Article 26 of the Charter, but has not dealt with the subject for more than two decades.

While the bilateral American-Soviet negotiations, such as those at SALT and other forums, have taken place outside of the United Nations, they are clearly within the purview of the world organization. The United Nations has discussed their subject matter throughout the negotiations and has consistently made pronouncements concerning them. They are, therefore, taken fully into account in this study.

Chapter 2

Past Efforts To Prevent Nuclear War

)

From the very beginning of the United Nations, its efforts were concentrated on the prevention of war and, above all, nuclear war. In addition to establishing an Atomic Energy Commission in January 1946 to promote the elimination of atomic weapons and all other weapons of mass destruction, the General Assembly, on 14 December 1946, adopted resolution 41(I), setting forth the Principles Governing the General Regulation and Reduction of Armaments. In that resolution, the Assembly recognized that early disarmament was necessary to strengthen international peace and security, and recommended the following: that the Security Council expedite the formulation of plans for the general regulation and reduction of armaments and armed forces; the consideration of conventions for prohibiting atomic and all other weapons of mass destruction; practical and effective safeguards by way of inspection and other means, and acceleration of the placing at its disposal the armed forces mentioned in Article 43 of the Charter.

As indicated earlier, no concrete progress was achieved and no agreements were concluded during the period of the Cold War. At the meetings of the Eighteen-Nation Disarmament Committee in Geneva beginning in 1962, however, the members discussed not only proposals for general and complete disarmament but also collateral measures for lessening international tension and improving confidence among states. It was in this area of limited or partial measures that the first agreements were concluded.

It is true that any agreements in the field of disarmament, whether they relate to small incremental measures of arms control or non-armament, which limit but do not reduce arms, or whether they serve to promote better communication and understanding or to reduce competition and tensions, serve to build confidence, increase international security, help to improve relations, and reduce the likelihood of war. So, of course, do agreements that settle international political disputes. In a sense, therefore, they can all be said to help to prevent conventional war and, thus, also serve to prevent nuclear war.

Some proposals and agreements, however, are aimed specifically at reducing or containing the risk of nuclear war, whether by accident, miscalculation or design. It is on these proposals, which relate more directly to the prevention of nuclear war, that the first section of this study concentrates.

REDUCING THE RISK
OF NUCLEAR WAR

Agreement On A Direct Communications Link
Between The Soviet Union And The
United States

Drawing on the experience of the Cuban Missile crisis, the United States proposed steps to reduce the risk of war by accident, miscalculation or failure of communications. One of the means for accomplishing that objective was the establishment of a direct communications link between Moscow and Washington for immediate use during times of crisis. The Soviet Union accepted the American proposal, and on 20 June 1963, after negotiations, the two parties signed a Memorandum of Understanding[4] establishing the direct communications link, which came to be known as "the Hot Line." The link consisted of two circuits by wire telegraph and by radiotelegraph.

This "Hot Line" agreement was the first bilateral agreement between the United States and the Soviet Union that gave recognition to the perils involved in possessing nuclear weapons, and it was a practical although limited step to reduce the risks inherent in those weapons.

The General Assembly, in resolution 1980(XVIII) adopted on 27 November 1963, expressed its satisfaction with the establishment of the direct communications link.

Advances in satellite communications technology and the desire to increase the reliability of the direct communications link as nuclear weapon systems became more sophisticated led to a desire to improve the link. Discussions were accordingly begun within the context of the SALT negotiations and resulted in an Agreement on Measures to Improve the USA-USSR Direct Communications Link[5], which was signed on 30 September 1971. This agreement provided for two additional circuits using satellite communications systems. Similar direct communication links were established between the Soviet Union and France in 1966, and between the Soviet Union and the United Kingdom in 1967.

Agreement on Measures to Reduce the Risk of Outbreak of Nuclear War Between the United States and the Union of Soviet Socialist Republics

Because a single nuclear weapon fired accidentally can inflict tremendous damage and provoke a similar response, it is essential to ensure that a nuclear war is not triggered by some accidental or unauthorized use of such a weapon. During the SALT negotiations, the United States and the Soviet Union decided to enter into arrangements to prevent misunderstandings and to reduce the risk of unintended nuclear war.

The two parties, therefore, agreed in 1971 on certain measures to reduce the risk of the outbreak of a nuclear war between them. This agreement, which came to be known as the "Nuclear Accidents Agreement,"[6] contains commitments by each party: (a) to maintain and improve its organizational and technical arrangements to guard against the accidental or unauthorized use of nuclear weapons; (b) to notify each other immediately in case of an accidental, unauthorized or other unexplained incident involving a possible detonation of a nuclear weapon, and to make every effort to render harmless or destroy such weapon without its causing damage; (c) to notify each other immediately on detection by missile warning systems of unidentified objects, or in case of signs of interference with these systems or related communications facilities; (d) to give advance notification of any planned launches that would extend beyond national territory in the direction of the other party; and (e) in other situations involving unexplained nuclear incidents, to act to reduce the possibility of its actions being misinterpreted by the other party.

Similar agreements to prevent the accidental or unauthorized use of nuclear weapons were entered into between the Soviet Union and France in 1976, and between the Soviet Union and the United Kingdom in 1977.

In the 1979 SALT II Treaty, the advance notification of missile launchings was extended to cover all planned multiple launches—that is, if two or more international missiles were in flight at the same time—even if they were not planned to extend beyond the party's national territory.

Agreement Between the United States and the Union of Soviet Socialist Republics on the Prevention of Incidents On or Over the High Seas

For a number of years, it has been customary for naval vessels and aircraft of the USSR and United States to follow and shadow each other on the high seas to obtain electronic and photographic intelligence. These activities sometimes led to incidents that verged on hostilities. The two parties, therefore, decided during the SALT negotiations to undertake preventive measures to ensure the safety of navigation of their naval forces and flight of their military aircraft over the high seas. In May 1972, at the time the SALT I treaties and agreements were concluded, the parties entered into an Agreement on the Prevention of Incidents On or Over the High Seas.[7] The agreement set forth a number of rules of conduct to ensure that the ships and aircraft of the two parties remained well clear of each other, and that ships and aircraft engaged in surveillance did not cause embarrassment or danger. The parties pledged not to permit their armed ships or aircraft to simulate attacks against those of the other party. They also agreed to provide advance notification of actions on the high seas that could be a danger to navigation or to aircraft and to exchange information about collisions, damage or other incidents at sea between the parties.

Agreement Between the United States and the Soviet Union on the Prevention of Nuclear War

In the aftermath of the SALT I treaties and agreements, when relations between the two powers were moving in the direction of detente, the two powers entered into discussions on how to further their objective of preventing a nuclear war and build on their previous agreements related to that goal. On the occasion of General Secretary Brezhnev's visit to the United States in June 1973, the two countries concluded a formal agreement on the Prevention of Nuclear War.[9]

In the agreement, the United States and the Soviet Union state that "an objective of their policies is to remove the danger of nuclear war and of the use of nuclear weapons." They agreed to act so as to prevent the development of situations capable of causing a dangerous exacerbation of their relations, to avoid military confrontations, and to exclude the outbreak of nuclear war between them and between either of them and other countries.

The parties agreed to proceed from the premise that each will refrain from the threat or use of force against the other, against the allies of the other party, and against other countries.

The parties also agreed that if relations between them or either of them and other countries, or between countries not parties to the Agreement, appear to involve the risk of nuclear war between the two parties or between either of them and other countries, they would immediately enter into urgent consultations to avert this risk. The progress and outcome of these consultations could be communicated to the United Nations and to allies and other governments.

The parties also agreed that nothing in the Agreement would affect the provisions of the United Nations Charter, including the inherent right of self-defense under the Charter, or alliance obligations.

The Agreement is of unlimited duration. The Agreement is noteworthy not merely because of its aim to prevent a nuclear war between them, which is obviously in the interest of each of them, but in particular because of its multilateral aspects. Its purpose is to prevent nuclear war "between either of the parties and other countries." Furthermore, although the undertaking against the threat or use of force is not as categorical as in Article 2(4) of the Charter, it is expressly stated to apply against allies of the other party and against other countries.

Since the consultations between the parties are to take place when relations between countries "not parties" to the Agreement involved the risk of nuclear war between either party and other countries, it may be that the parties had in mind avoiding the possibility of a local war involving the nuclear powers.,
/

The SALT II Joint Statement of Principles

At the time of the signing of the SALT II treaty and agreements in Vienna in June 1979, President Carter and General Secretary Brezhnev signed a Joint Statement of Principles and Basic Guidelines for Subsequent Negotiations on the Limitations of Strategic Arms.[10] Among the provisions agreed by them are the following:

Convinced that the early agreement on the further limitation and further reduction of strategic arms would serve to strengthen international peace and security and to reduce the risk of outbreak of nuclear war . . .

. . . the Parties will continue, for the purposes of reducing and averting the risk of outbreak of nuclear war, to seek measures to strengthen strategic stability by, among other things, limitations on strategic offensive arms most destablizing to the strategic balance and by measures to reduce and to avert the risk of surprise attack . . .

. . . the Parties will also consider further joint measures, as appropriate, to strengthen international peace and security and to reduce the risk of outbreak of nuclear war.

Significance of the Agreements

The foregoing agreements, all of which reflected and also helped to stimulate an improvement in relations between the United States and the Soviet Union, unquestionably do serve the purpose of reducing the risk of nuclear war even by design and intention, but more particularly as a result of accident, miscalculation or failure of communications.

They do not, however, remove the risk of nuclear war or assure its prevention. The parties still have not succeeded in reducing either the quantitative or qualitative nuclear arms race, nor have they given up their doctrines of nuclear deterrence, which are based on the readiness and willingness to use nuclear weapons. Moreover, each of the powers reserves the inherent right of self-defense under Article 51 of the Charter, which does not explicitly exclude the use of nuclear weapons. As was stated in paragraph 56 of the Final Document of the First Special Session on Disarmament: "The most effective guarantee against the danger of nuclear war and the use of nuclear weapons is nuclear disarmament and the complete elimination of nuclear weapons."

BANNING THE USE OF NUCLEAR WEAPONS

From the time of the explosion of the first atomic bomb, the nations of the world and the world community were preoccupied with efforts to deal with and eliminate the threat posed by nuclear weapons.

At the first meeting of the United Nations Atomic Energy Commission in June 1946, the United States proposed what came to be known as the "Baruch Plan"[11] for the international control of atomic energy. According to the Plan, all peaceful nuclear activities would be conducted under an International Authority, the manufacture of nuclear weapons would stop and, furthermore, nuclear weapons would be banned from national arsenals. Although the United States did not specifically call for a ban on the use of nuclear weapons, such a ban was implicit in its proposal.

The first specific proposal to ban the use of nuclear weapons was made by the Soviet Union at the next meeting of the Commission, when Ambassador Andrei Gromyko submitted a draft convention[12] whereby the parties would undertake not to use nuclear weapons in any circumstances, to prohibit the production and stockpiling of such weapons and to destroy all stocks of them.

The Soviet proposal was rejected, and the General Assembly in 1948 approved the Baruch Plan. Without Soviet support, however, the Plan could not be implemented and there began the long history of proposals, counter-proposals and protracted negotiations to ban the use of nuclear weapons and to reduce and eliminate them. Sometimes a proposal to ban the use of the weapons was put forward as a separate measure and, at other times, the ban on use was included as one item in a larger package of disarmament measures or in a comprehensive program.

For more than three decades, the Soviet Union took the initiative in submitting proposals from time to time, urging various forms of a total ban on the use of nuclear weapons, a ban on their first use, or a ban on their use against non-nuclear-weapon states. None of these proposals produced any concrete results, nor did those made at a later time by various non-aligned states, by China, and by others. Throughout these years, the United States, supported by the United Kingdom and France, opposed any absolute or unconditional ban on the use or first use of nuclear weapons, on the ground that the threat of their use or first use was necessary to deter an attack with conventional arms in which the Soviet Union was superior.

The positions of the United States and the Soviet Union seemed to be coming closer together in 1977 and 1978.

In October 1977, President Carter in the General Assembly pledged that, "the United States will not use nuclear weapons except in self-defense; that is, in circumstances of an actual nuclear or conventional attack on the United States, our territories or armed forces, or of such an attack on our allies." The pledge was repeated by Vice-President Mondale at the U. N. Special Session on Disarmament. This commitment, however, permits the use of nuclear weapons in response to a conventional attack by either a nuclear or non-nuclear power.

President Leonid Brezhnev went somewhat further when he stated on April 25, 1978 (and Foreign Minister Gromyko repeated at the Special Session) that the Soviet Union was "against the use of nuclear weapons; only extraordinary circumstances—aggression against our country or its allies by another nuclear power—could compel us to resort to this extreme means of self-defense." Thus the Soviet Union, like the United States, reserved the right of first use of nuclear weapons even in response to a conventional attack, but only if the attacker was a nuclear power. The insistence of these four nuclear powers on giving only a qualified or conditional undertaking was apparently based on their policies of maintaining the right to use these weapons as a deterrent to either nuclear or conventional attack.

Over the years, the question of the non-use of nuclear weapons has been considered by the United Nations in several different contexts, including a total ban on the use of these weapons, a convention on their prohibition, the non-use of force, the no-first-use of such weapons, their non-use against non-nuclear States, and their non-use against nuclear-free zones.

Because these different aspects of the problem of prohibiting the use of nuclear weapons are interrelated, the various proposals presented and resolutions adopted sometimes concentrated on a specific or limited aspect of the problem, depending upon the context, but often dealt with several aspects together. In an effort to bring some rationalization and clarity to a rather complex and sometimes confusing history, this study attempts to sort out the problem into its various elements and to deal with them separately, but some overlap has been unavoidable.

An Absolute Ban on the Use of Nuclear Weapons

The issue of banning the use of nuclear weapons had a prominent place in the discussions of the Sub-Committee of the Disarmament Commission, composed of Canada, France, the Soviet Union, the United Kingdom and the United States, which met in London from 1954 to 1957.

In June 1954, the Soviet Union included, in a proposal[13] submitted to the Sub-Committee on the basic provisions for an international disarmament convention, the following proposed undertaking:

As a first important step towards achieving complete elimination from the armaments of all States of atomic, hydrogen and other types of weapons of mass destruction, together with the simultaneous establishment of strict international control securing the observance of an agreement to prohibit the use of atomic energy for military purposes, the States concerned will assume a solemn and unconditional obligation not to use atomic, hydrogen or other weapons of mass destruction.

On the same day, France and the United Kingdom proposed a conditional prohibition of use, which permitted their use in defense against aggression. The first paragraph of the joint proposal[14] provided that:

The States members of the Sub-Committee regard themselves as prohibited in accordance with the terms of the Charter of the United Nations from the use of nuclear weapons except in defense against aggression. They recommend that the disarmament treaty should include an immediate and explicit acceptance of this prohibition by all signatory States, pending the total prohibition and elimination of nuclear weapons as proposed in the subsequent paragraphs of this memorandum. They further recommend that the obligations assumed by the Members of the United Nations to refrain in their international relations from the threat or use of force against the territorial integrity or political independence of any State should be accepted by all signatory States not members of the United Nations.

On 8 March 1955, Canada and the United States joined France and the United Kingdom in a proposal[15] submitted to the Sub-Committee

that all States possessing nuclear weapons should regard themselves as prohibited, in accordance with the terms of the Charter of the United Nations, from using such weapons, except in defense against aggression.

This formulation seemed to imply that the Charter permitted the use of nuclear weapons in defense against aggression. In addition, the four Western powers proposed a comprehensive disarmament program that provided for the total prohibition and elimination of nuclear weapons when all the agreed reductions of conventional armaments and armed forces had been completed.

On 19 April 1955, France and the United Kingdom submitted an amended proposal[16] whereby the total prohibition of use of nuclear weapons would come into force and their elimination would begin when 75 percent of the agreed reductions of conventional armaments and armed forces had been completed. This British and French modification marked the first time that any Western power had proposed an unconditional ban on use of nuclear weapons prior to their elimination.

On 10 May 1955, the Soviet Union submitted to the Sub-Committee a draft disarmament program[17] entitled "Reduction of Armaments, the Prohibition of Atomic Weapons, and the Elimination of the Threat of a New War," whereby it accepted the Anglo-French proposal that the total prohibition of use of nuclear weapons would come into force, and their elimination would begin, when 75 percent of the agreed reduction of conventional armaments and armed forces had been completed. The draft program also proposed the following:

Simultaneously with the initiation of measures for the reduction of the armaments and armed forces of the five Powers by the first 50 per cent of the agreed reduction to the prescribed levels and before the entry into force of the agreement on the complete prohibition of atomic weapons, States shall assume a solemn obligation not to use nuclear weapons, which they shall regard as prohibited to them. Exception to this rule may be permitted for purposes of defense against aggression, when a decision to that effect is taken by the Security Council.

This modification of the Soviet position was not regarded as significant by the Western powers since the Soviet Union could veto any decision of the Security Concil.

In August 1955, at a meeting of the Sub-Committee the Soviet Union introduced the proposal[18] made by Mr. N. A. Bulganin, Chairman of the Council of Ministers of the USSR, on 21 July 1955 at the Geneva Conference of the Heads of Government of the Four Powers:

At the same time, the Heads of Government of the Soviet Union, the United States, the United Kingdom and France, determined to prevent the use of atomic and hydrogen weapons, which are weapons of mass destruction of human beings, and to liberate the people from the threat of devastating atomic war, solemnly declare:

Pending the conclusion of the international convention for the reduction of armaments and the prohibition of atomic weapons, the Soviet Union, the United States, the United Kingdom and France assume the obligation not to be the first to use atomic or hydrogen weapons against any country and call on all other States to associate themselves with this declaration.

This was the first occasion on which any proposal for the renunciation of first use of nuclear weapons was introduced in the United Nations. On 30 April 1957, the Soviet Union reverted to the idea of a total ban and submitted to the Sub-Committee a proposal[19] for the reduction of armaments and armed forces and the prohibition of nuclear weapons. The proposal provided for an undertaking in the first stage to renounce the use of nuclear weapons of all types, including aerial bombs, rockets carrying atomic and hydrogen warheads irrespective of range, and atomic artillery.

Later that year, at the General Assembly, the Soviet Union submitted a draft resolution[20] which, among other measures, would have given priority to the prohibition of atomic weapons and their elimination and would have called upon States possessing nuclear weapons to assume, as a first step, an obligation not to use such weapons for a period of at least five years. The Soviet draft resolution was not adopted in the

First Committee.[21] This was the first occasion when a proposal for the non-use of nuclear weapons, submitted as an independent measure and not as part of a larger package, came to a vote in the United Nations.

The next development in the efforts to ban the use of nuclear weapons came from the initiative of a number of non-aligned countries. In 1961, at the 16th session of the General Assembly, a draft resolution was initiated by Ethiopia, which was cosponsored by eleven other African and Asian countries, calling for a declaration prohibiting the use of nuclear weapons and requesting the Secretary-General to conduct an inquiry into the possibility of convening a conference to sign a convention on the prohibition of the use of these weapons.

Italy submitted a number of amendments to the 12-Power text providing, in effect, a restatement of the traditional Western position for the prohibition of the use of nuclear and thermonuclear weapons only when "contrary to the Charter of the United Nations."

The United States opposed the 12-Power draft resolution on the ground that its aim could only be achieved by complete and controlled disarmament and that it sanctioned, by implication, other means of warfare. Both the United States and the United Kingdom maintained that the Charter right of individual and collective self-defense, including the right to determine the degree of force necessary to repel aggression, could not be abrogated.

The Soviet Union supported the draft resolution because it considered not only that the declaration would provide a good basis for the solution of the problem of the prohibition of the use of nuclear weapons but also that it would facilitate the implementation of general and complete disarmament.

After rejecting the Italian amendments, the Assembly, on 24 November 1961, adopted the draft resolution by 55 votes to 20, with 26 abstentions, as resolution 1653(XVI); it came to be known as the "Ethiopian resolution." The operative part of the resolution reads as follows:

1. *Declares* that:

(a) The use of nuclear and thermonuclear weapons is contrary to the spirit, letter and aims of the United Nations and, as such, a direct violation of the Charter of the United Nations;

(b) The use of nuclear and thermonuclear weapons would exceed even the scope of war and cause indiscriminate suffering and destruction to mankind and civilization and, as such, is contrary to the rules of international law and to the laws of humanity;

(c) The use of nuclear and thermonuclear weapons is a war directed not against an enemy or enemies alone but also against mankind in general, since the peoples of the world not involved in such a war will be subjected to all the evils generated by the use of such weapons;

(d) Any state using nuclear and thermonuclear weapons is to be considered as violating the Charter of the United Nations, as acting contrary to the laws of humanity and as committing a crime against mankind and civilization;

2. *Requests* the Secretary-General to consult the Governments of Member States to ascertain their views on the possibility of convening a special conference for signing a convention on the prohibition of the use of nuclear and thermonuclear weapons for war purposes and to report on the results of such consultation to the General Assembly at its seventeenth session.

Reports[22] by the Secretary-General showed 33 States favored the convening of a special conference for signing the proposed convention, 26 had negative views or doubts, and 3 States favored awaiting the results of the Conference of the Eighteen-Nation Committee on Disarmament. In November 1963, the Assembly, by resolution 1909 (XVIII), referred the matter to the Eighteen-Nation Committee on Disarmament for urgent consideration. The Soviet Union voted for the resolution; France, the United Kingdom, and the United States voted against it. In view of the basic disagreement among the nuclear powers, the discussions in the Committee were inconclusive.

In 1967, the Soviet Union submitted a draft convention to the General Assembly whereby the parties would undertake:

1. To refrain from using, or from threatening to use, nuclear weapons and from inciting other States to use them; and
2. To reach early agreement on ceasing production and destroying stockpiles of nuclear weapons, in conformity with a treaty on general and complete disarmament.

After much discussion, the Assembly in December 1967 adopted resolution 2289 (XXII), which was initiated by the Soviet Union and several non-aligned states, and contained the following:

1. *Expresses its conviction* that it is essential to continue urgently the examination of the question of the prohibition of the use of nuclear weapons and of the conclusion of an appropriate international convention;
2. *Urges* all States, in this connextion, to examine in the light of the Declara-

tion adopted by the General Assembly in resolution 1653 (XVI) the question of the prohibition of the use of nuclear weapons proposed by the Union of Soviet Socialist Republics and such other proposals as may be made on this question, and to undertake negotiations concerning the conclusion of an appropriate convention through the convening of an international conference, by the Conference of the Eighteen-Nation Committee on Disarmament, or directly between States . . .

The matter received little attention for a number of years thereafter, until it was raised by India at the first Special Session on Disarmament in June 1978. India revived the basic idea of the 1961 Ethiopian resolution (resolution 1653 (XVI). Since that time India has taken the lead in efforts to ban the use of nuclear weapons.

The Indian resolution was not pressed to a vote at the Special Session since it had been agreed that decisions there would be taken by consensus. India, however, reintroduced the draft resolution at the thirty-third annual regular session of the General Assembly in the fall of 1978, together with 33 cosponsors. It was adopted by a large majority (103 votes in favor, 18 against, and 18 abstentions) as resolution 33/71 B, entitled "Non-use of nuclear weapons and prevention of nuclear war." The United States reiterated its opposition to any absolute ban on the use of nuclear weapons and together with its allies voted "no"; the Soviet Union and its socialist allies, in a departure from their vote on the Ethiopian resolution seventeen years earlier, abstained; China did not participate.

The operative part of the resolution reads:

1. Declares that:

(a) The use of nuclear weapons will be a violation of the Charter of the United Nations and a crime against humanity;

(b) The use of nuclear weapons should therefore be prohibited, pending nuclear disarmament;

2. Requests all States, particularly nuclear-weapon States, to submit to the Secretary-General, before the 35th session of the General Assembly, proposals concerning the non-use of nuclear weapons, avoidance of nuclear war and related matters, in order that the question of an international convention or some other agreement on the subject may be discussed at that session.

Having received the proposals submitted by States to the 34th session, the Assembly transmitted them to the Committee on Disarmament for consideration. At its 35th session in 1980, resolution 35/152D, adopted by 112 votes to 19, with 14 abstentions, repeated the declarations in the 1978 resolution on the non-use of nuclear weapons and the prevention of nuclear war but added that the threat of use of nuclear weapons, as well as their use, should be prohibited.

At its 1981 session, the Assembly adopted resolution 36/92I, by 121 votes to 19, with 6 abstentions; it again repeated the declarations of the 1980 resolution, but requested that the forthcoming second special session on disarmament should consider the question of an international convention. This time the Soviet Union and its allies, who had abstained on the two previous similar resolutions, voted in favor; the United States and its allies again voted against the resolution.

At the Second Special Session in 1982 and again at the 1982 regular session of the General Assembly, India took a new step by presenting a draft convention on the prohibition of the use of nuclear weapons.

The Assembly adopted resolution 37/100C, initiated by India by a vote of 117 to 17, with 8 abstentions. It expressed the conviction that the prohibition of the threat or use of nuclear weapons would be a step towards their complete elimination leading to general and complete disarmament, and requested the Committee on Disarmament to undertake negotiations, on a priority basis, to achieve agreement on an international convention prohibiting the use or threat of use of nuclear weapons under any circumstances, taking as a basis the draft convention that was annexed to the resolution. China and the Soviet Union voted for the resolution; and France, the U. K. and the U. S. voted against.

While Assembly resolutions are not considered to be legally binding on the Member States, they do, of course, have both political and moral weight and add to the development of international law on the subject.

Non-Use of Nuclear Weapons and the Non-Use of Force

In 1972, at the 27th session of the General Assembly, the item "non-use of force in international relations and permanent prohibition of the use of nuclear weapons" was considered at the request of the Soviet Union. This was the first time that the prohibition of use of nuclear weapons was explicitly linked with the renunication of the use or threat of force, as proclaimed in the Charter.

The Assembly adopted resolution 2936 (XXVII), originally submitted by the Soviet Union and cosponsored by twenty-two other States, by a vote of 73 to 4 (including China), with 46 abstentions (including France, the United Kingdom and the United States).

The operative part of the resolution reads as follows:

1. Solemnly declares on behalf of the States Members of the Organization, their renunciation of the use or threat of force in all its forms and manifestations in international relations, in accordance with the Charter of the United Nations, and the permanent prohibition of the use of nuclear weapons;
2. Recommends that the Security Council should take, as soon as possible, appropriate measures for the full implementation of the present declaration of the General Assembly.

In 1976, at the initiative of the USSR, an item on the conclusion of a world treaty on the non-use of force in international relations was included in the agenda of the General Assembly. The item was allocated to the First Committee for its consideration with the understanding that later it would be referred to the Sixth Committee for examination of its legal implications. Under this item, the USSR submitted a draft World Treaty on the Non-use of Force in International Relations.[23]

At the same session, on the recommendation of the First Committee, the General Assembly adopted resolution 31/9 by which it invited Member States to examine further the above-mentioned draft Treaty and to communicate to the Secretary-General their views and suggestions on that subject.

At the 1977 session, on the recommendation of the Sixth Committee, the General Assembly decided to establish a Special Committee on Enhancing the Effectiveness of the Principle of the Non-Use of Force in International Relations with the goal of drafting a treaty. The Special Committee has reported on its work to succeeding sessions of the General Assembly, and its work is continuing.

The questions of the non-use of nuclear weapons and the non-use of force were also discussed at the 1978 Special Session on Disarmament. The Final Document of the Special Session dealt with them in as specific terms as were possible in view of the need to achieve a consensus. Paragraphs 57 and 58 state:

. . . the nuclear-weapon States have special responsibilities to undertake measures aimed at preventing the outbreak of nuclear war, and of the use of force in international relations, subject to the provisions of the Charter of the United Nations, including the use of nuclear weapons.
In this context, all States and in particular nuclear-weapon States should

consider as soon as possible various proposals designed to secure the avoidance of the use of nuclear weapons, the prevention of nuclear war and related objectives, where possible through international agreement, and thereby ensure that the survival of mankind is not endangered. All States should actively participate in efforts to bring about conditions in international relations among States in which a code of peaceful conduct of nations in international affairs could be agreed and which would preclude the use or threat of use of nuclear weapons.

No-first-use of Nuclear Weapons

When China exploded its first bomb on 16 October 1964, it issued a statement saying, "The Chinese Government solemnly declares that at no time and in no circumstances will China be the first to use nuclear weapons." It also formally proposed to the governments of the world, "That a summit conference of all the countries of the world be convened to discuss the question of the complete prohibition and thorough destruction of nuclear weapons, and that as the first step, the summit conference should reach an agreement to the effect that the nuclear powers and those countries which may soon become nuclear powers, neither to use them against non-nuclear countries and nuclear-free zones, nor against each other."[24]

After the Government of the People's Republic of China took its seat in the United Nations in 1971, it continued to repeat its pledge never to be the first to use nuclear weapons, and to urge the complete prohibition and thorough destruction of nuclear weapons. Nothing came of its earlier proposal for a summit conference, and China has not submitted any draft resolution in the United Nations either on a no-first-use pledge or on the prohibition and destruction of nuclear weapons.

In 1981, at the 36th session of the General Assembly, the Soviet Union, which had raised the subject in discussion on previous occasions, for the first time formally requested consideration of the question of no-first-use of nuclear weapons in an agenda item: "Declaration on the Prevention of Nuclear Catastrophe." The Assembly adopted resolution 36/100, initiated by the Soviet Union, by a vote of 82 to 19 (including France, the United Kingdom and the United States), with 41 abstentions. China did not participate in the vote.

The operative part of the resolution reads as follows:

Solemnly proclaims, on behalf of the States Members of the United Nations:

1. States and statesmen that resort first to the use of nuclear weapons will be committing the gravest crime against humanity;

2. There will never be any justification or pardon for statesmen who would take the decision to be the first to use nuclear weapons.

3. Any doctrines allowing the first use of nuclear weapons and any actions pushing the world towards a catastrophe are incompabible with human moral standards and the lofty ideals of the United Nations.

4. It is the supreme duty and direct obligation of the leaders of nuclear-weapon States to act in such a way as to eliminate the risk of the outbreak of a nuclear conflict. The nuclear-arms race must be stopped and reversed by joint efforts, through negotiations conducted in good faith and on the basis of equality, having as their ultimate goal the complete elimination of nuclear weapons.

5. Nuclear energy should be used exclusively for peaceful purposes and only for the benefit of mankind.

For further developments on the question of no-first-use of nuclear weapons and the unilateral Soviet declaration at the Second Special Session that it would not be the first to use nuclear weapons, see chapter 3 under the heading "Prevention of Nuclear War."

Non-use of Nuclear Weapons Against Non-Nuclear States

In the 1960s, when the world community was discussing the non-proliferation of nuclear weapons, questions arose about providing security guarantees or assurances to non-nuclear states, that is, states that did not possess nuclear weapons. Two kinds of such assurances were envisaged: "positive" security assurances, whereby the nuclear states would provide assistance and support to any non-nuclear state subjected to the threat or use of nuclear weapons against it, and "negative" security assurances, whereby the nuclear states would undertake not to use or threaten to use nuclear weapons against any state not possessing such weapons.

The provision of adequate security assurances to non-nuclear states was viewed by a number of countries as a critical element of an effective international regime to curb the spread of nuclear weapons. Such assurances would serve to allay the concern of non-nuclear states about the use or threat of use of nuclear weapons and thus would promote an international climate more propitious to the success of anti-proliferation efforts.

The question of security assurances, whether positive or negative in nature, was raised in the General Assembly on several occasions, but the Assembly could not agree on any formula for providing positive security assurances to non-nuclear states. However, in 1966, the Assembly adopted resolution 2153 (XXI), with the support of both the Soviet Union and the United States, which expressed the belief that the proliferation of nuclear weapons could lead to the aggravation of tensions between states and the risk of a nuclear war, and called for the conclusion of a treaty on the non-proliferation of nuclear weapons. The resolution also called on all nuclear Powers to refrain from the use, or threat of use, of nuclear weapons against states that conclude regional treaties for nuclear-weapon-freezones. It also called on the Eighteen-Nation Committee on Disarmament to consider the proposal that the nuclear Powers should give an assurance that they will not use, or threaten to use, nuclear weapons against non-nuclear states that had no nuclear weapons on their territories, and any other proposals for the solution of this problem.

The Treaty on the Non-Proliferation of Nuclear Weapons that was commended by the General Assembly on 12 June 1968, and was opened for signature on 1 July 1968, did not contain any provision for security assurances to non-nuclear states. Of the five nuclear powers, only the Soviet Union, the United Kingdom and the United States became parties to the Treaty.

However, on 19 June 1968, the Security Council adopted resolution 255 that was intended to provide positive security assurances to the non-nuclear states. The three nuclear powers and members of the Council, in accordance with their obligations under the Charter, promised to support any non-nuclear state that was the victim of attack or threats of aggression with nuclear weapons. The resolution was adopted by 10 votes to none, with 5 abstentions.

At the Review Conference of the Non-Proliferation Treaty in 1975, a number of states expressed the view that the positive security assurances contained in Security Council resolution 255 provided no greater assurances than already were contained in the Charter and were inadequate. The states pressed for specific negative security assurances.

Mexico, Romania and Yugoslavia, supported by a number of non-aligned states, submitted a draft resolution[25] proposing an additional protocol to the Non-Proliferation Treaty, whereby the U. S. S. R., the United Kingdom and the United States would undertake (a) never and under no circumstances to use or threaten to use nuclear weapons against non-nuclear parties to the treaty whose territories were completely free from nuclear weapons, and (b) refrain from the first use of nuclear weapons against other non-nuclear states parties to the Treaty.

Ghana, Nepal, Nigeria, Romania and Yugoslavia also sponsored a draft resolution[26] inviting the non-nuclear states on whose territories nuclear weapons were deployed not to allow their use or threat of use against other non-nuclear states parties to the Treaty.

Since the Conference had agreed to take decisions by consensus, in the absence of a consensus no decision was taken on either of the two draft resolutions, but they were reproduced in full in annex II of the Final Document of the Conference.

The consensus view of the Conference on these questions was set forth in the Final Declaration[27] as follows:

> The Conference urges all states, both nuclear-weapon states and non-nuclear-weapon states to refrain, in accordance with the Charter of the United Nations, from the threat or the use of force in relations between states, involving either nuclear or non-nuclear weapons. Additionally, it stresses the responsibility of all Parties to the Treaty and especially the nuclear-weapon states, to take effective steps to strengthen the security of non-nuclear-weapon states, and to promote in all appropriate fora the consideration of all practical means to this end, taking into account the views expressed at this Conference.

At its 1976 session, the General Assembly adopted resolution 31/189C, which had been proposed by Pakistan, requesting the nuclear-weapon states, as a first step towards a complete ban on the use or threat of use of nuclear weapons, to consider undertaking, without prejudice to their obligations arising from treaties establishing nuclear-weapon-free zones, not to use or threaten to use nuclear weapons against non-nuclear-weapon states not parties to the nuclear security arrangements of some nuclear-weapon Powers. China voted in favor, while France, the Soviet Union, the United Kingdom, and the United States abstained.

At the 1978 Special Session of the General Assembly devoted to disarmament, the question of security assurances to non-nuclear states was dealt with mainly in the context of the discussions on the non-proliferation of nuclear weapons and on nuclear-weapon-free zones.

Among the nuclear powers, only China clearly and unequivocally declared that it would never use nuclear weapons against any non-nuclear state. The other nuclear powers persistently refused to make such statements despite strong pressure from the non-nuclear states, but they did clarify their positions.

The Soviet Union announced that it had signed Protocol II to the

Treaty of Tlatelolco by which it undertook to respect the status of the zone and not to use nuclear weapons against any country that was a member of the Latin-American nuclear-free zone. It also declared that it would "never use nuclear weapons against those states which renounce the production and acquisition of such weapons and do not have them on their territories."

It also announced that it was prepared to enter into bilateral agreements to that effect with any such non-nuclear states.

The United States and the United Kingdom gave more limited undertakings. The U. S. declaration was:

> The United States will not use nuclear weapons against any non-nuclear-weapon state party to the Non-Proliferation Treaty or to any comparable internationally binding commitment not to acquire nuclear explosive devices, except in the case of an attack on the United States, its territories or armed forces or its allies by such a state allied to a nuclear-weapon state or associated with a nuclear-weapon state in carrying out or sustaining the attack.

The U. K. declaration, which was similar to the American, was as follows:

> I accordingly give the following assurance, on behalf of my Government, to non-nuclear-weapon states which are parties to the Non-Proliferation Treaty or to other internationally binding commitments not to manufacture or acquire nuclear explosive devices: Britain undertakes not to use nuclear weapons against such States except in the case of an attack on the United Kingdom, its dependent territories, its armed forces or its allies by such a state in association or alliance with a nuclear-weapon state.

All three pledges were designed to encourage non-nuclear states to adhere to or abide by the provisions of the Non-Proliferation Treaty (NPT). Some of the non-nuclear states felt that the United States and United Kingdom declarations were discriminatory against non-nuclear states that were not parties to the NPT but that had no nuclear weapons on their territories.

France made a more restricted pledge. It stated that a decision by the states of a region to preserve a nuclear-free status should entail an obligation for nuclear-weapon states not to seek a military advantage from the situation and, in particular, should preclude any use or threat of the use of nuclear weapons against the non-nuclear countries and nuclear-free zones.

China, reiterating its position never to be the first to use nuclear weapons and in favor of a non-use agreement, said that, in the absence of such an agreement, a measure of urgency was for all nuclear countries to undertake not to resort to the threat or use of nuclear weapons against the non-nuclear countries and nuclear-free zones.

The Final Document of the Special Session reached consensus on a call for strengthening the security of non-nuclear states in both the Declaration and the Programme of Action, as follows:

32. All States, in particular nuclear-weapon states, should consider various proposals designed to secure the avoidance of the use of nuclear weapons and the prevention of nuclear war . . .

59. In the same context, the nuclear-weapon states are called upon to take steps to assure the non-nuclear weapon states against the use or threat of use of nuclear weapons. The General Assembly notes the declarations made by the nuclear-weapon states and urges them to pursue efforts to conclude, as appropriate, effective arrangements to assure non-nuclear-weapon states against the use or threat of use of nuclear weapons.

At the regular 1978 session of the General Assembly, the Soviet Union proposed the elaboration of a convention on strengthening guarantees of the security of non-nuclear states, whereby the nuclear-weapon states would pledge not to use or threaten to use nuclear weapons against non-nuclear states that renounce the production and acquisition of nuclear weapons and have no nuclear weapons in their territory or anywhere under their jurisdiction or control. Pakistan proposed a counter-draft convention whereby the nuclear weapon states would pledge not to use or threaten to use nuclear weapons against non-nuclear weapon states not parties to the nuclear security arrangements of some nuclear-weapon states, and whereby the nuclear-weapon states would undertake to achieve the complete elimination of nuclear weapons in the shortest possible time.

The United States and its NATO allies were opposed to both proposals. The United States contented itself with suggesting that the Security Council merely endorse the limited pledges made by the three nuclear powers at the Special Session in the spring of 1978.

The Soviet Union and Pakistan agreed to a compromise. Both revised their draft resolutions to request that the Committee on Disarmament consider all the proposals made, without assigning priority to any. Both resolutions were adopted by overwhelming majorities with the United States voting in favor of the Soviet draft. China voted against the Soviet draft and together with France voted for the Pakistani resolution on which the United States and the Soviet Union abstained.

These votes reflect different approaches to the problem and presage the lack of progress in the Committee on Disarmament. From 1979 to date, the matter has been discussed in the Committee, where the consensus rule also prevails, without significant progress.

Nuclear-weapon-free Zones

The concept of nuclear-free zones was developed in the late 1950s and 1960s when nations of the world became concerned by the spread of nuclear weapons to additional countries both by deployment of the weapons in non-nuclear countries and by the possible acquisition or manufacture of such weapons by non-nuclear countries. The spread of nuclear weapons was regarded as increasing the risks of nuclear war.

In addition, non-nuclear countries in different regions of the world considered that their establishment of nuclear-free zones would enable them to prevent the nuclear arms race from spreading to their areas either by the testing or deployment of nuclear weapons by the existing nuclear powers or by the acquisition of such weapons by countries in their region.

Perhaps most important of all, the sponsors of proposals for nuclear-free zones saw it as an important way to ensure that their countries would be freed from the possible use or threat of use of nuclear weapons against them.

The first proposal for a nuclear-free zone was launched by Poland in 1958 when it published a memorandum,[28] which came to be known as the "Rapacki Plan." The plan consisted of a proposal for the creation of a nuclear-free zone in Central Europe, covering Poland, Czechoslovakia, East and West Germany, and for the prohibition of use of nuclear weapons against the countries comprising the zone. The plan went through several revisions in an effort to make it acceptable to the Western powers, but the latter opposed all versions of the plan on the grounds that they were intended to reduce Western nuclear strength in Europe and would give the Soviet Union a military advantage because of its superiority in conventional arms. Nothing came of the plan.

In 1961, on the initiative of a number of African states that were aroused by the explosion of a nuclear weapon in Algeria in 1960 by France, the General Assembly adopted resolution 1652 (XVI). It called on States to refrain from testing, storing, or transporting nuclear weapons in Africa, and to consider and respect the continent as a denuclearized zone. In 1964, the first Summit Conference of the Organization of African Unity issued a solemn Declaration on the Denuclearization of Africa. In 1965, the General Assembly adopted resolution 2033 (XX), which endorsed the 1964 Declaration on the Denuclearization of Africa and called on all States to respect the continent of Africa as a nuclear-free zone. The resolution also expressly called on all States to refrain from the use, or threat of use of nuclear weapons on the continent and hoped that the African States would take steps through the Organization of African Unity to implement the declaration.

In 1974, the General Assembly unanimously adopted resolution 3261E (XXIX) that again called on all states to refrain from testing, manufacturing, deploying, transporting, storing, using or threatening to use nuclear weapons on the African continent.

Thereafter, each year the Assembly has adopted a resolution on the Implementation of the Declaration on the Denuclearization of Africa. Up to the present time, however, no treaty creating a nuclear-free zone in Africa has as yet been considered and no steps have been taken to provide for the implementation of the 1964 Declaration.

The first, and indeed so far the only, successful effort to establish a nuclear-free zone in an inhabited area of the earth was the creation of the nuclear-free zone in Latin America in 1967 by the Treaty for the Prohibition of Nuclear Weapons in Latin America, commonly known as the "Treaty of Tlatelolco."

A number of Latin American states, concerned by the Cuban Missile Crisis of October 1962 and fearing that their region might become involved in the nuclear strategies and rivalries of the Soviet Union and the United States, decided to propose the denuclearization of Latin America. In 1963, the General Assembly adopted resolution 1911 (XVIII) expressing its support for and encouragement of the idea.

After intensive and complex negotiations, which were reported annually to the United Nations, and which were assisted by a technical consultant appointed by the Secretary-General, the Treaty for the Prohibition of Nuclear Weapons in Latin America was signed in the borough of Tlatelolco in Mexico City in 1967.

The Treaty bans the testing, use, manufacture, acquisition, storage, installation, deployment, and any form of possession, directly or indirectly, of nuclear weapons in the zone. In addition to providing for the total absence of nuclear weapons from the zone, Protocol II to the Treaty requires that the Treaty "shall be fully respected . . . in all its express aims and provisions" by the nuclear powers, who also "undertake not to use or threaten to use nuclear weapons against the Contracting Parties of the Treaty."

The Treaty was welcomed by General Assembly resolution 2286 (XXII) as "an event of historic significance" and the Assembly invited the nuclear powers to sign and ratify Protocol II as soon as possible.

Each year thereafter the Assembly called on the nuclear powers who had not yet signed and ratified Protocol II to do so.

Protocol II has been signed and has entered into force for all five nuclear Powers.[29] The Treaty of Tlatelolco is therefore the first and only disarmament treaty imposing limitations on the testing, deployment or use of nuclear weapons that has binding force on all the nuclear powers.

On signing Protocol II each of the nuclear powers made a statement:[30]

China stated that it will never use or threaten to use nuclear weapons against non-nuclear Latin American countries and the nuclear-free zone and that for Latin America to become a true nuclear-weapon-free zone, all nuclear countries, and particularly the superpowers, must undertake not to use or threaten to use nuclear weapons against the Latin American countries.

France stated that it interprets the Protocol as not restricting the full exercise of the right of self-defense enshrined in Article 51 of the United Nations Charter.

The Soviet Union stated that, if any party to the Treaty committed an act of aggression with the support of a nuclear-weapon state, or if any nuclear-weapon states took any actions incompatible with their obligations under the Protocol, it reserved the right to review its obligations under the Protocol.

The United Kingdom stated that, if any party to the Treaty carried out an act of aggression with the support of a nuclear-weapon state, it would be free to reconsider the extent to which it would be committed by the Protocol.

The United States stated that it would consider that an armed attack by a party to the Treaty, in which it was assisted by a nuclear-weapon state, would be incompatible with the party's obligations under the Treaty.

It will be noted that these reservations are narrower and more limited in scope, that is, they give less freedom of action to the nuclear powers, than the qualified negative security assurances that the five nuclear powers were prepared to give to non-nuclear states.[31]

Prior to the successful conclusion of the Treaty of Tlatelolco, there had been other proposals, apart from those for Central Europe and for Africa, for the establishment of nuclear-free zones.

Such zones had been proposed for the Balkans by Romania, for Asia and the Pacific by China, for the Mediterranean by the Soviet Union, and for the Nordic countries by Finland. None of these proposals became the subject of United Nations action.

The Treaty of Tlatelolco and the Indian explosion of a peaceful nuclear device in 1974, stimulated greater interest in the concept of a nuclear-free zone and resulted in several new initiatives. In addition to revised interest in the African zone, new proposals were put forward for the establishment of such zones in the Middle East by Iran and Egypt, in South Asia by Pakistan, and in the South Pacific by New Zealand. Resolutions favoring the establishment of each of these zones were adopted by the General Assembly. In the case of Africa, the Middle East, and South Asia, the Assembly has adopted resolutions annually since 1974.

Up to the present time, however, no formal negotiations have begun and no concrete or significant progress has been made for the establishment of nuclear-free zones in any of these areas. Some of the difficulties and problems in connection with the creation of nuclear-free zones are discussed in a Special Report[32] prepared by governmental experts, which was submitted by the Conference of the Committee on Disarmament to the General Assembly in 1975, pursuant to the request of the General Assembly in resolution 3261F (XXIX). The Conclusions of the Report stated that circumstances in different regions vary so widely that a pragmatic and flexible approach would be needed in each case. While favoring the establishment of nuclear-free zones, the Report indicated a number of areas where the experts did not agree concerning the obligations that should be assumed by the parties and by the nuclear powers. There was no agreement on the scope and nature of the assurances by nuclear powers not to use or threaten to use nuclear weapons against any member of the zone. Some experts maintained that clear and formal assurances by nuclear-weapon states not to use or threaten to use nuclear weapons against any member of a nuclear-weapon-free zone was an essential factor for the effectiveness of the zone. Other experts felt that while such an undertaking could enhance the effectiveness of the zone, this question should not be regarded as a prerequisite but considered at the time a particular zone agreement would be negotiated. The view was also expressed that one of the considerations to be taken into account was whether, in specific cases, the provision of non-use assurances could be seen as undercutting existing positive assurances, for example, to non-nuclear allies of a nuclear power. Most experts, however, felt that the nuclear-weapon states should pledge themselves to respect the nuclear-weapon-free status of a zone and not to use, or threaten to use nuclear weapons against any state in a zone.[33]

At the 1975 session of the General Assembly, Mexico introduced a draft resolution cosponsored by non-aligned states which would, *inter alia*, provide for the definition of the principal obligations of the nuclear-weapon states towards a nuclear-weapon-free zone. It defined as one obligation the need to refrain from using or threatening to use nuclear weapons against states in the zone. The draft was adopted as resolution 3472 (XXX). China voted in favor of the resolution. France, the United Kingdom and the United States voted against, expressing difficulty about accepting such an obligation before concrete negotiations would start for the establishing of a nuclear-weapon-free zone. The U. S. S. R. abstained in the vote.

The Final Document of the Special Session on Disarmament supported the establishment of nuclear-free zones and summarized the consensus of views as follows:

60. The establishment of nuclear-weapon-free zones on the basis of arrangements freely arrived at among the states of the region concerned, constitutes an important disarmament measure.

61. The process of establishing such zones in different parts of the world should be encouraged with the ultimate objective of achieving a world entirely free of nuclear weapons. In the process of establishing such zones, the characteristics of each region should be taken into account. The states participating in such zones should undertake to comply fully with all the objectives, purposes and principles of the agreements or arrangements establishing the zones, thus ensuring that they are genuinely free from nuclear weapons.

62. With respect to such zones, the nuclear-weapon states in turn are called upon to give undertakings, the modalities of which are to be negotiated with the competent authority of each zone, in particular:

(a) to respect strictly the status of the nuclear-weapon-free zone;

(b) to refrain from the use or threat of use of nuclear weapons against the states of the zone.

CESSATION OF THE NUCLEAR ARMS RACE AND NUCLEAR DISARMAMENT

As mentioned previously, the United Nations, from the beginning of its efforts to maintain international peace and security, sought to avoid a nuclear arms race and to eliminate nuclear weapons in order to prevent a nuclear war.

These aims were formally expressed in the Preamble to the 1968 Non-Proliferation Treaty, which has obtained the adherence of more parties (117) than any other disarmament treaty. The Preamble of the Treaty includes the following:

> *Considering* the devastation that would be visited upon all mankind by a nuclear war and the consequent need to make every effort to avert the danger of such a war and to take measures to safeguard the security of peoples,
>
> *Believing* that the proliferation of nuclear weapons would seriously enhance the danger of nuclear war . . .
>
> *Declaring* their intention to achieve at the earliest possible date the cessation of the nuclear arms race and to undertake effective measures in the direction of nuclear disarmament . . .
>
> *Recalling* the determination expressed by the Parties to the 1963 Treaty banning nuclear weapon tests in the atmosphere, in outer space and under water in its Preamble to seek to achieve the discontinuance of all test explosions of nuclear weapons for all time and to continue negotiations to this end,
>
> *Desiring* to further the easing of international tension and the strengthening of trust between states in order to facilitate the cessation of the manufacture of nuclear weapons, the liquidation of all their existing stockpiles, and the elimination from national arsenals of nuclear weapons and the means of their delivery pursuant to a treaty on general and complete disarmament under strict and effective international control.

Article VI of the Treaty made the pursuit of an end to the nuclear arms race and of nuclear disarmament binding obligations. It states:

> Each of the Parties of the Treaty undertakes to pursue negotiations in good faith on effective measures relating to cessation of the nuclear arms race at an early date and to nuclear disarmament, and on a treaty on general and complete disarmament under strict and effective international control.

It was generally accepted that the cessation of the nuclear arms race would require, among other steps, the cessation of the testing of nuclear weapons.

A Nuclear Test Ban

No other question in the field of disarmament has occupied as much of the attention of the United Nations as that of stopping nuclear-weapon tests. It has been a prime objective of the world community since 1954 when Prime Minister Jawaharlal Nehru of India called for a "standstill agreement" to halt nuclear testing. It has been a separate agenda item of the General Assembly every year since 1957, and the Assembly has adopted more than three dozen resolutions calling for an end to nuclear testing, which is far more than on any other disarmament item. In one way or another these resolutions repeatedly and urgently called for an end to all testing.

Many proposals have been put forward over the years to achieve or make progress towards a comprehensive test ban. They include various forms of suspension of testing; unilateral or mutual moratoria on testing; a "threshold" above which all underground tests would be banned; a progressive lowering of any agreed temporary threshold; and interim steps to reduce the number and magnitude of tests until they were completely phased out. None of the proposals led to a solution.

Throughout this period the United States has maintained that verification of underground nuclear tests was not possible without a sufficient number of on-site inspections, while the Soviet Union has maintained that all nuclear testing could be effectively verified by technical means without on-site inspection. In 1962 and 1963, however, the Soviet Union stated its willingness to accept two or three on-site inspections a year to verify compliance with an underground test ban. The United States, however, insisted that a minimum of seven on-site inspections per year would be necessary for effective verification of underground tests. Most of the nations of the world thought that each of the two powers could accept the proposal of the other without doing any damage to its interests, and that their rigidity in refusing to accept the other side's proposal, or to reach a compromise, reflected a greater desire to continue testing than to reach an agreement to stop testing.

The United States and the United Kingdom proposed on a number of occasions that, as a first step pending agreement on verification of underground testing, the Soviet Union should agree to halt the testing of nuclear weapons in the atmosphere, in outer space, and under water, which could be verified by national means without the necessity for any international system of verification. For several years the Soviet Union rejected the proposal, but in June 1963 it announced that it was willing to negotiate a treaty on those lines. The three powers met in Moscow on 15 July and rapidly agreed to a partial test ban treaty that was signed on 5 August 1963.

The first treaty dealing with nuclear weapons was the Partial Test Ban Treaty of 1963. This treaty banned all nuclear tests in the atmosphere, in outer space, and under water, but did not prohibit underground tests except for any such test that released radioactive debris that travelled beyond the borders of the state conducting the explosion.

The treaty was negotiated and signed by the Soviet Union, the United Kingdom, and the United States and is of unlimited duration. It has more than 100 parties but the other two nuclear powers, China and France, have refused to become parties on the ground that they are far behind the two nuclear superpowers both in testing and in the production of nuclear weapons. After suits were initiated by Australia and New Zealand in the International Court of Justice, however, France decided of its own accord to stop testing in the atmosphere and for several years has conducted only underground tests.

The Partial Test Ban Treaty was the first world-wide agreement in the field of nuclear disarmament. It was hailed as an historic event that would, in addition to stopping the further nuclear pollution of the atmosphere, help to restrain the nuclear arms race. The treaty, however, did not, in fact, serve to curb the nuclear arms race; underground nuclear testing proceeded at a greater rate after the treaty than before. More than twice as many underground tests have been carried out in the twenty years since the signing of the treaty than in the eighteen years before it was concluded. The treaty has turned out to be more of an environmental and health measure than a disarmament measure.

Despite the commitment of the three nuclear powers who negotiated the Partial Test Ban Treaty to continue negotiations for a comprehensive test ban, which commitment was reaffirmed in the 1968 Non-Proliferation Treaty, no negotiations in fact took place for a decade.

In 1974, however, the Soviet Union and the United States negotiated and signed the Threshold Test Ban Treaty[34] that banned any underground nuclear-weapon test having a yield in excess of 150 kilotons (the equivalent of 150,000 metric tons of TNT), and each of the parties agreed to limit the number of its underground tests to a minimum. They also agreed to continue negotiations for the cessation of all underground tests. The treaty has not been ratified and has not entered into force but the two parties have agreed to abide by its terms.

In 1976, the two powers also signed the Peaceful Nuclear Explosions Treaty,[35] which banned any individual underground explosion having a yield in excess of 150 kilotons and any group explosion (consisting of a number of individual explosions) having an aggregate yield exceeding 1,500 kilotons. This treaty, too, has not been ratified and has not entered into force, but the two parties again agreed to abide by its terms.

In 1977, the two powers announced that they and the United Kingdom would begin negotiations in July on a comprehensive test ban treaty. These trilateral negotiations proceeded in private but the parties presented joint progress reports to the Committee on Disarmament from time to time indicating that considerable progress had been made in the negotiations but that some difficult problems remained. The last report was submitted on 31 July 1980.[36] The trilateral negotiations were suspended in 1980.

The Group of 21 (mainly non-aligned countries) of the Committee for Disarmament proposed the establishment of a Working Group of the Committee to commence concrete negotiations for a comprehensive test ban without waiting for the conclusion of the trilateral negotiations. In 1979, the General Assembly, by resolution 34/73, requested the Committee to initiate negotiations on a treaty as a matter of the highest priority. The Soviet Union was sympathetic to the creation of the Working Group, but the United Kingdom and the United States were opposed. In the absence of a consensus in the Committee, the Working Group could not be created and, despite the frustrations felt by the Group of 21, the Committee was not able to commence any specific negotiations for a comprehensive test ban treaty.

At the 1978 Special Session on Disarmament, many Member States were disappointed at the failure of the trilateral negotiations to agree on a comprehensive test ban treaty, which many had hoped would be concluded in time for presentation to the Special Session. The delegations had to content themselves with the following statement in the Final Document:

> The cessation of nuclear-weapon testing by all states within the framework of an effective nuclear disarmament process would be in the interest of mankind. It would make a significant contribution to the above aim of ending the qualitative improvement of nuclear weapons and the development of new types of such weapons and of preventing the proliferation of nuclear weapons. In this context the negotiations now in progress on a 'treaty prohibiting nuclear-weapon tests, and a protocol covering nuclear explosions for peaceful purposes, which would be an integral part of the treaty,' should be concluded urgently and the result submitted for full consideration by the multilateral negotiating body with a view to the submission of a draft treaty to the General Assembly at the earliest possible date.

> All efforts should be made by the negotiating parties to achieve an agreement which, following General Assembly endorsement, could attract the widest possible adherence. In this context, various views were expressed by non-nuclear-weapon states that, pending the conclusion of this treaty, the world community would be encouraged if all the nuclear-weapon

states refrained from testing nuclear weapons. In this connection, some nuclear-weapon states expressed different views.

In response to a request by the General Assembly in 1979 (decision 34/422), the Secretary-General undertook a study by consultant experts of the question of a comprehensive nuclear test ban. The experts reached the following among other conclusions:[37]

151. A main objective of all efforts of the United Nations in the field of disarmament has been to halt and reverse the nuclear-arms race, to stop the production of nuclear weapons and to achieve their eventual elimination.

152. In this connexion, a comprehensive test ban is regarded as the first and most urgent step towards a cessation of the nuclear-arms race, in particular, as regards its qualitative aspects.

153. Over the years, enormous efforts have been invested in achieving a cessation of all nuclear-weapon tests by all States for all time . . .

154. The trilateral negotiations have now been going on for nearly three years, while in the Committee on Disarmament negotiations have still not commenced. In order to bring the achievement of a comprehensive test ban nearer to realization, much more intensive negotiations are essential. Verification of compliance no longer seems to be an obstacle to reaching agreement.

155. A comprehensive test ban could serve as an important measure of non-proliferation of nuclear weapons, both vertical and horizontal.

156. A comprehensive test ban would have a major arms limitation impact in that it would make it difficult, if not impossible, for the nuclear-weapon states parties to the treaty to develop new designs of nuclear weapons and would also place constraints on the modification of existing weapon designs.

157. A comprehensive test ban would also place constraints on the further spread of nuclear weapons by preventing nuclear explosions . . .

158. In the view of the parties to the non-proliferation Treaty, a comprehensive test ban would reinforce the Treaty by demonstrating the awareness of the major nuclear Powers of the legal obligation under the Treaty 'to pursue negotiations in good faith on effective measures relating to cessation of the nuclear arms race at an early date.'

159. The arms limitation benefits of a comprehensive test ban could be enhanced, and the channels of arms competition among the great Powers further narrowed, if the comprehensive test ban

were followed by restrictions on the qualitative improvement of nuclear delivery vehicles.

160. To achieve its purpose, the comprehensive test ban must be such as to endure. With the passage of time, even non-parties to the comprehensive test ban may feel inhibited from engaging in nuclear-weapon testing . . . ."

In forwarding the report to the Committee on Disarmament in the spring of 1980, the Secretary-General stated:

In my first statement to the Conference of the Committee on Disarmament in 1972, I stated the belief that all the technical and scientific aspects of the problems had been so fully explored that only a political decision was necessary in order to achieve agreement. I still hold that belief. The problem can and should be solved now.

The failure of the three nuclear states to agree on a comprehensive test ban treaty, or even to the establishment of a Working Group by the Committee on Disarmament to commence multilateral negotiations to elaborate a treaty text, was the subject of much adverse comment by non-nuclear states at the Second Review Conference of the Parties to the Non-Proliferation Treaty held in Geneva in the summer of 1980. The Group of 77 (approximately 125 developing countries of the Third World) criticized the nuclear powers for not implementing the provisions of the treaty, in particular its Article VI whereby they committed themselves to seek a "cessation of the nuclear arms race at an early date." They considered that Article VI had remained largely a dead letter for the entire ten years since the conclusion of the treaty.

The main demand of the Group of 77 countries with respect to disarmament was their call for multilateral negotiations for a test ban treaty to start in the Committee of Disarmament in the beginning of 1981 and, pending the conclusion of a treaty, the proclamation by the nuclear powers of an immediate moratorium on all their nuclear weapon tests.

The non-nuclear delegations to the Conference seemed to be convinced that concrete and significant progress in nuclear disarmament was urgent in order to ensure the continued strength and effectiveness of the Non-Proliferation Treaty. At the top of their list of nuclear disarmament measures is a comprehensive test ban.

The unwillingness of the nuclear powers to make any real concessions on this main demand, as well as on other aspects of nuclear disarmament, resulted in the failure of the Review Conference. Unlike the 1975 Review Conference, the second one ended without the adoption of any substantive final declaration, and without even any formal reaffirmation of support for the Non-Proliferation Treaty.

In the autumn of 1980, the General Assembly adopted two resolutions on a comprehensive test ban. The first, resolution 35/145A, which was sponsored by Mexico and nine other non-aligned states, noted that the experts report had emphasized that non-nuclear states in general had come to regard the achievement of a comprehensive test ban as a litmus test of the determination of the nuclear states to halt the arms race, and also that verification of compliance no longer seemed an obstacle to reaching agreement. The resolution then, *inter alia*, urged the members of the Committee on Disarmament to support the creation of a working group which should begin early in 1981 multilateral negotiations for a treaty to ban all nuclear-weapon tests, and called on the three nuclear powers, to halt all nuclear testing either through agreed or unilateral moratoria as a provisional measure until the treaty enters into force. The vote on the resolution was 111 to 2 (United Kingdom and United States), with 31 abstentions (including China, France and the Soviet Union).

The second resolution (35/145B) was originally sponsored by Australia and six Western states, and incorporated a number of significant amendments by Sweden and three other non-aligned states. It expressed the conviction that a comprehensive test ban treaty is a vital requirement to halt the nuclear arms race and the qualitative improvement of nuclear weapons and to prevent their spread to additional countries; it requested the Committee on Disarmament to initiate substantive negotiations on a comprehensive test ban treaty as a matter of the highest priority at the beginning of 1981 so that it could submit the treaty to the second special session on disarmament to be held in 1982. The vote on this resolution was 129 to none, with 16 abstentions (including all five nuclear powers).

With the election of a new Administration in the United States, the American position, which had previously always supported a comprehensive test ban but had considered the problem of adequate verification of compliance with an underground test ban as the main obstacle to agreement, underwent an important change. At the 1981 session of the General Assembly, the United States stated[38] that it supported the "long term goal" of halting nuclear tests, but "international conditions ... are not now propitious for immediate action on this worthy project." On 9 February 1982, the United States announced[39] in the Committee on Disarmament, "While a comprehensive ban on nuclear testing remains an element in the full range of long-term United States arms control objectives, we do not believe that, under present circumstances, a comprehensive test ban could help to reduce the threat of nuclear weapons or to maintain the stability of the nuclear balance."

At its 1981 session, the General Assembly again adopted two resolutions (36/84 and 36/85) on a comprehensive test ban, essentially similar to those adopted in 1980. This time, however, there were a large number of affirmative votes and fewer abstentions since the Soviet Union and its allies voted for both resolutions, rather than abstaining as they had in 1980. The United Kingdom and the United States were alone in voting against the non-aligned resolution, and they, together with China and France, abstained on the Western resolution. China and France explained their abstentions on the grounds that a nuclear test ban was an integral part of the process of disarmament and was linked to other measures of nuclear disarmament that, moreover, required the reduction of the nuclear weapons stockpiles of the two superpowers.

The 1982 Second Special Session on Disarmament failed to reach any agreed consensus on substantive matters of disarmament, either nuclear or conventional. Given the changed position of the United States concerning a comprehensive test ban, there was no possibility of any agreement in that regard.

While the members of the United Nations were disappointed and frustrated by the change in the United States position, they were again surprised and taken aback when the United States confirmed[40] on 20 July 1982 that President Reagan had decided not to resume the trilateral negotiations on a comprehensive test ban treaty because of doubts about the verifiability of a test ban and because of the need to keep testing new nuclear weapons.

At the 1982 regular session of the General Assembly, in addition to the usual approaches to the question by a group of non-aligned states and by a group of Western states, the Soviet Union adopted a separate approach calling for the immediate cessation and prohibition of nuclear-weapon tests and presented a document containing "Basic provisions of a treaty on the complete and general prohibition of nuclear-weapon tests." The General Assembly adopted three resolutions on the subject.

Resolution 37/72 on "Cessation of all test explosions of nuclear weapons" was introduced by Mexico. The resolution briefly summarized the background to the question and stressed that, on seven different occasions in the more than forty resolutions on the subject, the Assembly had condemned nuclear-weapon tests in the strongest terms, and that the continuance of testing would intensify the arms race and increase the danger of nuclear war. It also reaffirmed that a comprehensive test ban treaty is a matter of the highest priority and is vital to prevent both vertical and horizontal proliferation of nuclear weapons; it urged the Soviet Union, the United Kingdom and the United States to abide strictly by their obligations under the Partial Test Ban Treaty and the Non-Proliferation Treaty to continue negotiations to end all tests for all time and, as a provisional measure, to stop all nuclear test explosions either through a trilaterally-agreed moratorium or through three unilateral declarations; and it called on the members of the Committee on Disarmament to establish immediately an *ad hoc* working group for the multilateral negotiation of a treaty prohibiting all nuclear-weapon tests, and to endeavor to submit the text of such a treaty to the next session of the General Assembly. The Soviet Union voted for the resolution the United Kingdom and the United States cast the only two negative votes, and China and France abstained.

Resolution 37/73 on "Urgent need for a comprehensive test ban treaty" was introduced by Australia. The resolution, while not as strong and categorical in its terms as the previous one and while not calling for a moratorium on testing, was similar to it in many ways. It also reiterated grave concern that nuclear testing continued unabated despite the express wishes of the overwhelming majority of states, and that a ban on all nuclear tests by all states for all time was of the greatest urgency and highest priority and was vital to halt and reverse the nuclear arms race and the spread of nuclear weapons; it noted that the Committee on Disarmament had established an *ad hoc* working group to define issues relating to vertification and compliance with a nuclear test ban; it requested the Committee to take steps to initiate substantive negotiations so that a comprehensive test ban treaty could be submitted to the General Assembly at the earliest possible date; and finally it requested the Committee to determine the arrangements necessary for an international seismic monitoring network and an effective verification system. The United States cast the only negative vote, and China, France, the Soviet Union and the United Kingdom abstained.

Resolution 37/85 on "Immediate cessation and prohibition of nuclear-weapon tests" was introduced by the Soviet Union. The resolution expressed deep concern over the continuing nuclear arms race and the growing danger of nuclear war and the conviction that the immediate cessation and prohibition of all nuclear-weapon tests by all states would be a serious obstacle to the development of new nuclear weapons and the emergence of new nuclear states. It urged the Committee on Disarmament to begin negotiations to elaborate a draft treaty on the complete and general prohibition of nuclear-weapon tests and referred to the Committee the basic provisions of such a treaty, the text of which was annexed to the resolution; in addition, it called on all nuclear-weapon states, in order to create favorable conditions for drafting such a treaty, not to conduct any nuclear explosions as from a date agreed upon until the treaty was concluded. The Soviet Union was the only nuclear-weapon state to vote for the resolution, and China, France, the United Kingdom and the United States cast the only negative votes.

While it is clear that by far the overwhelming number of countries strongly favor a complete ban on nuclear-weapon tests at the earliest date, first by the Soviet Union, the United Kingdom and the United States, it is not likely to be realized in the foreseeable future because of opposition by the United Kingdom and the United States. This is all the more apparent because of the decision of the United States not to resume the trilateral negotiations for a treaty.

The failure to pursue negotiations for a comprehensive test ban and the resulting impossibility of achieving such a ban is a severe set-back to the efforts for the cessation of the nuclear arms race and for nuclear disarmament. It is also a blow to the efforts to prevent the proliferation of nuclear weapons and to prevent a nuclear war.

Non-Proliferation of Nuclear Weapons

As has been mentioned previously, the Member States of the United Nations have from the earliest days exerted efforts to avoid a nuclear arms race. They believed that the proliferation of nuclear weapons would seriously enhance the danger of nuclear war. By "proliferation" they meant both "vertical" proliferation, that is, the further development, production and deployment of nuclear weapons by the nuclear powers, and "horizontal" proliferation, that is, the spread of nuclear weapons to non-nuclear states.

Two approaches to dealing with the problem have already been discussed—by banning the testing of nuclear weapons and by the creation of nuclear-free zones. A third, direct approach to preventing the spread of nuclear weapons to additional countries was first raised in the General Assembly by Ireland, which put forward relevant proposals in each year from 1958 to 1961.

In 1961, the General Assembly unanimously approved the Irish proposal in resolution 1665 (XVI), which called on all states to conclude an international agreement whereby the nuclear states would refrain from transmitting information to non-nuclear states for their manufacture, and non-nuclear states would not manufacture or otherwise acquire control of such weapons.

The draft outlines of treaties for general and complete disarmament, submitted by the Soviet Union and the United States to the Eighteen-Nation Committee on Disarmament in 1962, each contained provisions, among the first stage measures, to prevent the dissemination or acquisition of nuclear weapons. In 1965, each of the two powers submitted to the Committee on Disarmament draft treaties on the non-proliferation of nuclear weapons.

In the same year, the General Assembly adopted resolution 2028 (XX), which had been co-sponsored by the eight non-aligned members of the Committee on Disarmament. The resolution called for the early conclusion of a non-proliferation treaty based, *inter alia,* on "an acceptable balance of mutual responsibilities and obligations of the nuclear and non-nuclear powers."

After protracted negotiations, the United States and the Soviet Union, in 1967, submitted to the Committee on Disarmament identical but separate draft treaties.[41] In 1968, these were replaced by a joint American-Soviet draft treaty, which contained several revisions that would strengthen the obligations of the nuclear powers to seek a cessation of the nuclear arms race at an early date.

After a thorough debate the joint draft treaty was approved by resolution 2373 (XXII) of the General Assembly on 12 June 1968. As regards Article VI, containing the pledge to seek a cessation of the nuclear arms race and for nuclear disarmament, the measures most frequently suggested for top priority were: a comprehensive test ban, a cut-off of production of fissionable materials, a convention on the prohibition of use of nuclear weapons, cessation of the production of nuclear weapons, and elimination of their stockpiles.

As explained previously,[42] on 19 June 1968, the Security Council adopted resolution 255, which was intended to provide "positive" security assurances to non-nuclear states that were parties to the Non-Proliferation Treaty.

The Treaty was opened for signature on 1 July 1968, and entered into ty, but without China and France. Among the non-nuclear powers, several states that might be considered as near-nuclear or as potential nuclear powers are also not parties—including Argentina, Brazil, India (which had conducted a peaceful nuclear explosion in 1974), Israel, Pakistan, South Africa and Spain.
nuclear explosion in 1974), Israel, Pakistan, South Africa and Spain.

At the first Review Conference on the Non-Proliferation Treaty in 1975, dissatisfaction was expressed by many non-nuclear parties to the treaty over the failure of the nuclear powers to implement the obligations they had assumed in the treaty. Nevertheless, the Conference was able to adopt a Final Declaration by consensus, which reaffirmed the strong support of the parties for the Treaty and for non-proliferation, and urged greater efforts by the nuclear powers to carry out all their treaty commitments. Although the Declaration was adopted by consensus, the Group of 77 participants attached an "interpretative statement" whereby they reaffirmed their views on ending nuclear testing, on the drastic reduction of nuclear arsenals and on security assurances to the non-nuclear parties to the treaty.[43]

In the years following the 1975 Review Conference, the General Assembly adopted several resolutions emphasizing the responsibility of the two major nuclear powers with regard to the treaty, in particular, the need to bring about the cessation of the nuclear arms race and to undertake effective measures of nuclear disarmament. Such measures include a comprehensive test ban, calling for negative security assurances to non-nuclear states and for greater international cooperation in utilizing nuclear energy for peaceful purposes.

During this period, there was growing criticism by Members of the United Nations of the failure of the nuclear powers to carry out the provisions of the treaty and to halt and reverse the nuclear arms race. Disappointment and frustration were repeatedly expressed at the lack of success in concluding a comprehensive test ban treaty. In addition, the differences of view among some non-nuclear states that were not parties to the treaty, which they regarded as discriminatory, and between those nuclear powers that were and those that were not parties to the treaty, explain the paucity of treatment accorded to the question of nuclear non-proliferation in the Final Document of the 1978 first Special Session on Disarmament. Its provisions were limited to calling for effective measures to "minimize the danger" of proliferation and for full implementation of all the provisions of the Non-Proliferation Treaty and the Treaty of Tlatelolco, and to expressing the hope that adherence to those treaties would continue to increase.

When the second Review Conference of the Non-Proliferation Treaty was convened in the summer of 1980, it soon became apparent that the non-nuclear parties were not prepared to condone further the failure of the nuclear parties to live up to their obligations under the treaty and, in particular, as regards the cessation of the nuclear arms race. Not only had the nuclear powers not succeeded in achieving a comprehensive test ban, which is generally regarded as the single most important non-proliferation measure, but there was a renewed upward spiral in the nuclear arms race. It seemed likely that the 1979 SALT II Treaty would not be ratified, since on 3 January 1980 President Carter requested the United States Senate to postpone debate on it "in the light of the Soviet invasion of Afghanistan." Moreover, the non-nuclear powers made plain their feelings that the nuclear powers had largely ignored the Final Declaration of the 1975 Review Conference.

As mentioned earlier,[44] under the heading "A Nuclear Test Ban," the unwillingness of the nuclear powers to make any meaningful concession with regard to the negotiation of a comprehensive test ban treaty by the Committee on Disarmament led to the failure of the Review Conference. It ended without the adoption of any substantive final declaration or even any formal reaffirmation of the importance of and support for the Non-Proliferation Treaty.

The failure of the Review Conference has led to fears that there may be some weakening of support for the Non-Proliferation Treaty and of hopes for a cessation of the nuclear arms race. These fears have been increased by the decision of the United States in July 1982 not to resume the trilateral negotiations for a comprehensive test ban.[40]

If indeed there has been some erosion in the credibility or viability of the Non-Proliferation Treaty, then efforts to prevent the proliferation of nuclear weapons and thereby increase the risk of nuclear war would be undermined. As the Preamble to the Treaty declares, "the proliferation of nuclear weapons would seriously enhance the danger of nuclear war."

The SALT Process

When the Non-Proliferation Treaty was signed on 1 July 1968, it was announced by the Soviet Union and the United States that agreement had been reached to enter into bilateral discussions on the limitation and the reduction of both offensive strategic nuclear weapons delivery systems and systems of defense against ballistic missiles. These bilateral discussions came to be known as the Stretegic Arms Limitation Talks, or SALT.

In the Introduction to his Annual Report on the Work of the Organization for 1968-1969,[45] the Secretary-General warned that the development of anti-ballistic missiles (ABMs) and multiple independently-targetable reentry vehicles (MIRVs) could lead to greater insecurity and destabilization of the existing rough balance and would accelerate the "mad momentum" of the nuclear arms race until it ended in unmitigated disaster for all. He appealed for the immediate beginning of the SALT negotiations. Pending progress in the talks, he urged a freeze on the development and deployment of offensive and defensive strategic nuclear weapons either by agreement or by unilateral moratoria declared by both sides.

At the 1969 session of the General Assembly, it was announced that the talks would begin on 17 November 1969. The Assembly adopted resolution 2602A (XXIV), which took up the Secretary-General's suggestion and appealed to the Soviet Union and the United States "to agree, as an urgent preliminary measure, on a moratorium on further testing and deployment of new offensive and defensive strategic nuclear-weapon systems."

The two nuclear powers, however, opposed the resolution on the ground that any outside interference might hamper the successful development of the talks, but they abstained on the vote.

After two and one-half years of negotiations, the first round of the talks (SALT I) were successfully concluded on 26 May 1972 at a summit meeting in Moscow. President Nixon and General Secretary Brezhnev signed the ABM Treaty and the Interim Agreement on strategic offensive arms.

The ABM Treaty was of unlimited duration with a right of withdrawl on six months' notice. The parties considered that limiting ABMs would be a "substantial factor in curbing the race in strategic offensive arms and would lead to a decrease in the risk of outbreak of war involving nuclear weapons." The Treaty provided that each party could have two limited deployment areas, one to protect its capital and another to protect an intercontinental ballistic missile (ICBM) launching site. Limitations were placed on the development of new and improved ABMs, which would be restricted to a single warhead.

The Interim Agreement on Strategic Offensive Arms and the Protocol to it provided that the United States and the Soviet Union could not build any additional fixed land-based ICBM launchers beyond those already in existence or under construction (1054 for the United States and 1418 for the U. S. S. R.) or convert launchers for light ICBMs to heavy ones. The number of submarine-launched ballistic missiles (SLBMs) was fixed at 710 launchers on 44 ballistic missile submarines for the United States and 950 launchers on 62 submarines for the Soviet Union. The Agreement was concluded for an initial five year period (since renewed) and the parties agreed to continue negotiations for a more comprehensive agreement.

Both the ABM Treaty and the Interim Agreement were to be verified by "national technical means," (that is, by surveillance satellites and other remote national sensors) and a Standing Consultative Commission was established to consider and resolve questions of compliance and other relevant matters.

At the 1974 summit meeting in Moscow, the parties signed a Protocol to the ABM Treaty limiting each party to only one area, either to defend its national capital, as in the case of the Soviet Union, or to defend an ICBM site, as in the case of the United States. In fact, the United States did not even proceed with the completion of its sole ABM system near Grand Forks, North Dakota.

In November 1974, at a summit meeting in Vladivostok, President Ford and General Secretary Brezhnev agreed on the basic framework for the SALT II agreement. The Vladivostok accord provided that each party could have up to a total limit of 2400 strategic nuclear delivery vehicles (ICBMs, SLBMs and heavy bombers). Of this number

1320 could have MIRV systems, but no new land-based ICBMs could be built.

The SALT II negotiations resumed in Geneva in 1975. The lengthy negotiations led to the conclusion, at a summit meeting in Vienna in June 1979 between President Carter and General Secretary Brezhnev, of the SALT II Treaty and Agreements.

The SALT II Treaty (Treaty on the Limitation of Strategic Offensive Arms) is a complex one which provides for:

an equal aggregate limit of 2250 strategic delivery vehicles by the end of 1981.

an equal aggregate limit of 1320 launchers with MIRVed ballistic missiles and heavy bombers with cruise missiles, of which no more than 1200 could be launchers of MIRVed ballistic missiles (ICBMs and SLBMs)

an equal aggregate limit of 820 launchers of MIRVed ICBMs

In addition to these numerical limits, the Treaty provided for other limitations, the most important of which are:

no increase in the number of fixed ICBM launchers or heavy launchers

a ban on heavy mobile ICBM launchers and on heavy launchers of SLBMs and ASBMs (air to surface ballistic missiles)

only one new type of ICBM could be flight-tested or deployed by each party

a ban on increasing the number of warheads on existing ICBMs, with a limit of 10 warheads on the one new type of ICBM permitted for each party, a limit of 14 warheads on SLBMs, and 10 on ASBMs. Long-range cruise missiles on each heavy bomber would be limited to an average of 28, and on existing types of bombers to 20

limits on the launch weight and throw weight of ballistic missiles and a ban on converting light ICBMs to heavy ones

a ban on Soviet SS-16 ICBMs, which could be confused with SS-20s, and on rapid reload ICBM systems

a ban on long-range ballistic missiles on surface ships, and on ballistic and cruise missile launchers on the seabeds or beds of internal waters

advance notification of certain ICBM test launchings

Verification of the Treaty is to be by national technical means and the parties agreed not to interfere with the other's means of verification or to impede them by concealment or by denial of telemetric information.

The Treaty is to remain in force through 1985.

By a Protocol to the Treaty, the parties banned the deployment of mobile ICBM launchers and of ground and sea-based cruise missiles capable of ranges above 600 kilometers, and banned the flight-testing and deployment of ASBMs. The Protocol was to expire on 31 December 1981.

In a Joint Statement of Principles,[10] the parties agreed to "continue, for the purposes of reducing and averting the risk of outbreak of nuclear war, to seek measures to strengthen strategic stability by, among other things, limitations on strategic offensive arms most destabilizing to the strategic balance and by measures to reduce and avert the risk of surprise attack." They agreed that the further measures would be verified by national technical means and "cooperative measures" to strengthen verification and the work of the Standing Consultative Commission.

They also agreed to pursue substantial reductions in the number of strategic offensive arms and their qualitative limitation, including restrictions on the development, testing, and deployment of new types or modernization of existing weapons, and to resolve the issues that were included in the Protocol.

Finally, they agreed to consider other steps to enhance strategic stability, to ensure equality and equal security of the parties, and to consider further joint measures to strengthen international security and reduce the risk of outbreak of nuclear war.

During the discussion of the SALT II treaty in the General Assembly in 1979, both the Soviet Union and the United States stated that they viewed the treaty as a major contribution to averting a nuclear war and to the strengthening of detente. They also renewed their commitments to achieving further limitations and deeper reductions. The United Kingdom, and most of the United Nations Members, welcomed the treaty as a start towards real nuclear disarmament. France considered the treaty as an important step and hoped it would enter into force soon; but France and China both stated that they would join the process of reducing nuclear arms only after substantial reductions in the nuclear arsenals of the two major nuclear powers.

The Assembly adopted without a vote resolution 34/87F, initiated by 8 non-aligned states, which called for the early entry into force of the treaty and welcomed the agreement by the two powers to pursue negotiations for substantial reductions of and qualitative limitations on strategic armaments.

The following year, the General Assembly adopted resolution 35/156K, again without a vote, which deplored the fact that the SALT II treaty had not yet been ratified and called for its early entry into force. It also urged the two parties in the meantime to refrain from any act that would defeat the object and the purpose of the treaty.

On 3 January 1980, President Carter requested the U. S. Senate, "In light of the Soviet invasion of Afghanistan . . . that you delay consideration of the SALT II treaty." President Reagan regarded the treaty as flawed and, before and after his election, opposed its ratification. Hence the prospects for its entry into force are increasingly remote. Nevertheless, both President Carter and President Reagan have declared their intentions to abide by the provisions of the treaty as long as the Soviet Union does so, and General Secretary Brezhnev has made a similar statement regarding Soviet intentions.

Irrespective of the fate of the SALT II treaty, the pronouncement on the SALT process by the 1978 Special Session on Disarmament remains valid. It states:

The Union of Soviet Socialist Republics and the United States of America should conclude at the earliest possible date the agreement they have been pursuing for several years in the second series of the strategic arms limitation talks (SALT II). They are invited to transmit in good time the text of the agreement to the General Assembly. It should be followed promptly by further strategic arms limitation negotiations between the two parties, leading to agreed significant reductions of, and qualitative limitations on, strategic arms. It should constitute an important step in the direction of nuclear disarmament and ultimately of establishment of a world free of such weapons.

Cessation of the Production of Nuclear Weapons and the Reduction and Elimination of Their Stockpiles

At the 1978 Special Session on Disarmament, many proposals were presented on various aspects of halting the nuclear arms race and on the elements of nuclear disarmament. After much discussion and negotiation, agreement was finally reached on Paragraph 47 of the Final Document, which states that:

Nuclear weapons pose the greatest danger to mankind and to the survival of civilization. It is essential to halt and reverse the nuclear arms race in all its aspects in order to avert the danger of war involving nuclear weapons. The ultimate goal in this context is the complete elimination of nuclear weapons.

The Programme of Action dealt with the way to achieve that goal, which was set out in what has been described as "the famous paragraph 50" as follows:

The achievement of nuclear disarmament will require urgent negotiation of agreements at appropriate stages and with adequate measures of verification satisfactory to the States concerned for:

(a) cessation of the qualitative improvement and development of nuclear-weapons systems;

(b) cessation of the production of all types of nuclear weapons and their means of delivery, and of the production of fissionable material for weapons purposes;

(c) a comprehensive phased programme with agreed time-frames, whenever feasible for progressive and balanced reduction of stockpiles of nuclear weapons and their means of delivery, leading to their ultimate and complete elimination at the earliest possible time.

Consideration can be given in the course of the negotiations to mutual and agreed limitation or prohibition, without prejudice to the security of any State, of any types of nuclear armaments.

At the 33rd regular session of the General Assembly later that year, it adopted resolution 33/71H, which had been initiated by a group of non-aligned states, concerning the implementation of the nuclear disarmament provisions of the Final Document. The resolution, *inter alia*, urged all the nuclear states to proceed to consultations regarding early negotiations on halting the nuclear arms race and on progressive and balanced reduction of nuclear weapons and their means of delivery leading to their complete elimination. It also recommended that the Disarmament Commission consider the nuclear arms race and nuclear disarmament in order to expedite negotiations for the elimination of the danger of a nuclear war. China and the Soviet Union voted in favor, but France, the United Kingdom, and the United States abstained.

The following year, the Soviet Union initiated a resolution requesting the Committee on Disarmament to consider "Nuclear weapons in all aspects" and to begin negotiations on the cessation of the nuclear arms race and nuclear disarmament in accordance with the Final Document. The resolution was adopted as number 34/83J. France and the United States voted against it, the United Kingdom abstained and China did not participate.

In 1980, the Soviet Union again initiated a resolution on the cessation of the nuclear arms race and nuclear disarmament that noted with alarm the increased risk of nuclear catastrophe due to the intensification of the nuclear arms race and the adoption of the new doctrine of the limited use of nuclear weapons. The Soviet Union called on the Committee on Disarmament as a matter of priority to undertake consultations on establishing an *ad hoc* working group on the cessation of the nuclear arms race and nuclear disarmament. The resolution was adopted as number 35/152B, with France, the United Kingdom and the United States voting against and China not participating.

A non-aligned resolution (35/152C) also urged the Committee on Disarmament to establish an *ad hoc* working group on the same subject. China and the Soviet Union voted in favor, and France, the United Kingdom and the United States voted against.

In 1981, a draft resolution introduced by the German Democratic Republic, again entitled "Nuclear weapons in all aspects," was adopted by the Assembly as resolution 36/92E. The resolution called for negotiations on the cessation of the production of nuclear weapons and on their gradual reduction until total destruction, and for consideration in the first stage of the cessation of the development and deployment of new types and systems of nuclear weapons. It also again called for the establishment of the *ad hoc* working group. France, the United Kingdom, and the United States voted against, and China did not participate.

In 1982, the General Assembly again adopted a similar resolution (37/78C), which noted with alarm that to the doctrine of a limited nuclear war (that is, a nuclear war that could be limited in area or scope) there was added the concept of a protracted nuclear war. It called on the Committee on Disarmament to proceed with negotiations on the cessation of the nuclear arms race and nuclear disarmament, to elaborate a nuclear disarmament program, and to establish for this purpose an *ad hoc* working group. Once again, France, the United Kingdom, and the United States voted against and China did not participate.

It is thus amply clear that the general membership of the United Nations favors the commencement of negotiations for the cessation of the nuclear arms race and nuclear disarmament, but their repeated calls for this and for the establishment by the Committee on Disarmament of a working group for that purpose have gone unheeded.

Since the Committee on Disarmament also conducts its work by consensus, it is not possible for decisions to be taken on either substantive or procedural matters in the absence of a consensus. The opposition of the major Western powers made it impossible to implement the foregoing resolutions, even as regards the establishment of an *ad hoc* working group on nuclear disarmament, nor did the discussions on substance make any progress. The matter is still unresolved at the time of writing.

Other Measures of Nuclear Disarmament

Throughout its existence, the General Assembly has supported, urged or recommended a large number of different measures in the field of nuclear disarmament. Some of these measures have resulted in the conclusion of international treaties.

Three treaties have been signed and have entered into force that limit the areas in which nuclear weapons can be tested or deployed. They are:

the 1959 Antartic Treaty,[46] which bans any nuclear explosions or disposal of radioactive waste material in Antartica, and provides for the complete demilitarization of the area and its use for peaceful purposes only;

the Outer Space Treaty[47] of 1967, which bans the placing in orbit around the earth any carriers of nuclear weapons or other weapons of mass destruction, the installation of such weapons on celestial bodies or stationing them in outer space in any other manner. The moon and other celestial bodies are to be used exclusively for peaceful purposes

the Seabed Treaty[48] of 1971, which prohibits the emplacement of nuclear weapons or other weapons of mass destruction on or in the seabed or ocean floor beyond a 12-mile coastal zone.

Each of these treaties sought to prevent the introduction of nuclear weapons into areas that were previously free of them, and thus, in effect, created nuclear-free zones, although in regions that are unpopulated. As such, they do play some role, albeit limited, in reducing the risks of the outbreak of nuclear war.

Over the years, a large number of proposals for limiting, containing, and ending the nuclear arms race and reducing the threat of nuclear weapons has been presented to the General Assembly. Only a few of them, less than two dozen in all, as outlined in this study, have resulted in binding international treaties or agreements.

Several hundred Assembly resolutions, however, have set forth the views of the world community on many aspects of the arms race and disarmament. As has been noted, while these resolutions are not considered to be legally binding, they do have considerable political and moral weight and have a role in the development of international law. They help to create a climate of opinion, to establish standards of conduct, and to define the goals to be pursued in relation to halting the arms race and averting the threat of war and, in particular, of nuclear war. It is noteworthy that over the years the number of resolutions adopted by the General Assembly in this field has increased steadily. For example, in the first 30 years of the United Nations, from 1946 to 1975, the Assembly adopted 212 resolutions, while in the last seven years, from 1976 to 1982, the Assembly adopted 327 resolutions.

The most important of the declarations and recommendations made by the General Assembly relating to the subject of this study, which have not been discussed in greater detail under specific headings, are summarized here.

In 1957, the General Assembly adopted resolution 1148 (XII) to give priority to reaching an agreement providing for six partial measures of disarmament, including three measures of nuclear disarmament: the immediate suspension of nuclear weapon testing with prompt installation of effective international control; the cessation of the production of fissionable materials for weapons purposes; and the reduction of stocks of nuclear weapons through a program of transfer of stocks of fissionable material from weapons use to non-weapons uses.

Beginning in 1971, the General Assembly, on the initiative of Sri Lanka, has each year adopted a resolution to establish the Indian Ocean as a zone of peace. By resolution 2832 (XXVI), the Assembly solemnly declared the Indian Ocean for all time as a zone of peace. It called upon the Great Powers to enter into consultations with the littoral states with a view to halting the further expansion of the military presence of the Great Powers in the Indian Ocean and to eliminating all bases, military installations, the disposition of nuclear weapons and other weapons of mass destruction, and any manifestation of Great Power military rivalry. It also called upon the littoral and hinterland states, the permanent members of the Security Council, and other major maritime users of the Indian Ocean to pursue a system of universal collective security without military alliances and to help ensure that warships and military aircraft would not use the Indian Ocean for any threat or use of force contrary to the United Nations Charter. Despite taking the following actions: establishment of a continuing *Ad Hoc* Committee on the Indian Ocean; the preparation of a factual study by the Secretary-General on the Great Powers' military presence in the Indian Ocean; the holding of bilateral talks on the subject between the Soviet Union and the United States (which led to no result); the endorsement of the concept by the 1978 Special Session on Disarmament; the convening of a Meeting of the Littoral and Hinterland States of the Indian Ocean in 1979 that resulted in a set of principles including the denuclearization of the zone; and continuing efforts to convene a conference on the Indian Ocean; the implementation of the declaration establishing a zone of peace is no nearer achievement at the present time, and indeed may be further away, than it was twelve years ago. Although all the nuclear powers now participate in the work of the *Ad Hoc* Committee and resolutions of the General Assembly on the subject are now adopted by consensus, the deterioration in the international political and security climate has meant the indefinite postponement of the establishment of the Indian Ocean as a zone of peace.

In 1978, the General Assembly adopted resolution 33/91F, on the initiative of the Soviet Union, calling on the nuclear-weapon states to refrain from stationing nuclear weapons on the territories of states where there are no nuclear weapons, and calling on all non-nuclear-weapon states that had no nuclear weapons on their territory to refrain from any steps that would result in the stationing of such weapons. The resolution was opposed by the NATO powers. In each of the years thereafter, the Assembly adopted similar resolutions. In 1980 and subsequent years, it requested the Committee on Disarmament to undertake talks to elaborate an international agreement on the subject of non-stationing of nuclear weapons. In 1982, it also called on the nuclear-weapon states to freeze qualitatively nuclear weapons on the territories of other states. In view of the opposition of the United States and its allies, no progress has been made towards implementing these resolutions.

In 1978, the General Assembly adopted resolution 33/91H, initiated by Canada, on the prohibition of the production of fissionable material for weapons purposes. The resolution requested the Committee on Disarmament, at an appropriate stage of its implementation of the Final Document of the Special Session on Disarmament, to consider urgently a verified cessation and prohibition of the production of fissionable material for nuclear weapons and other nuclear explosive devices. The United States voted for the resolution and the Soviet Union voted against it. In each of the years thereafter, the Assembly adopted similar resolutions, but in 1982 the United States and the Soviet Union both abstained in the voting. In 1979, the resolution also considered that such cessation of production of fissionable material and the progressive conversion and transfer of stocks to peaceful purposes would be a step towards halting and reversing the nuclear arms race, and the prohibition of such production would facilitate the prevention of nuclear proliferation. Up to the present time, because of the lack of support by the nuclear powers, no progress has been made.

In 1981, the General Assembly adopted resolution 36/92K, initiated by the German Democratic Republic, requesting the Committee on Disarmament to begin negotiations to conclude a convention on the prohibition of the production, stockpiling, deployment and use of neutron weapons. The resolution was a follow-up of a draft convention submitted by the Soviet Union to the Committee on Disarmament in 1978 that had been discussed in the General Assembly that year in the more general context of the prohibition of the development and manufacture of new types of weapons of mass destruction. A similar resolution was adopted by the General Assembly at its 1982 session. Because of the opposition of the United States and its allies, no progress has been made.

OTHER EFFORTS TO PROMOTE NUCLEAR DISARMAMENT

In the previous section "Cessation of the Nuclear Arms Race and Nuclear Disarmament" we have discussed the agreements and treaties concluded and the many declarations and recommendations that have been made on specific measures of nuclear disarmament. In addition to action on these concrete measures of disarmament, the General Assembly has also made recommendations on what might be described as disarmament-facilitating measures. These are actions that would tend to facilitate the cessation of the nuclear arms race and promote the achievement of nuclear disarmament. They include the preparation of expert studies by the Secretary-General that would lead to a better understanding of different aspects of the problems of nuclear weapons and nuclear disarmament, to attempts to elaborate measures or instruments that would create greater confidence among nations and thus lessen the risk of the outbreak of war and also to facilitate progress towards nuclear disarmament. In this section we shall discuss the decisions of the General Assembly of this type that are intended to pave the way to agreement on measures of nuclear disarmament.

Studies by the Secretary-General

The Secretary-General, at the request of the General Assembly, has undertaken a number of expert studies on various aspects of the arms race and of disarmament. While all of them are relevant to the problem of war and peace, the present study deals only with those having some direct relationship to the problem of nuclear weapons and nuclear war.

The first study in the field of nuclear weapons was undertaken by a group of experts in 1967, on the initiative of the Secretary-General himself, and had the rather formidable title of "Effects of the Possible Use of Nuclear Weapons and the Security and Economic Implications for States of the Acquisition and Further Development of These Weapons." The unanimous report[49] of the experts was endorsed by the Secretary-General and the General Assembly, in resolution 2342A, expressed its satisfaction with the report as an authoritative statement. In their conclusions, the experts stated:

The solution of the problem of ensuring security cannot be found in an increase in the number of states possessing nuclear weapons or, indeed, in the retention of nuclear weapons by the powers currently possessing them. An agreement to prevent the spread of nuclear weapons as recommended by the United Nations, freely negotiated and genuinely observed, would therefore be a powerful step in the right direction, as would also an agreement on the reduction of existing nuclear arsenals. Security for all countries of the world must be sought through the elimination of all stockpiles of nuclear weapons and the banning of their use, by way of general and complete disarmament.

. . . But it must be realized that the measures of arms limitation, however, desirable, cannot of themselves eliminate the threat of nuclear conflict. They should be regarded not as ends sufficient in themselves but only as measures which could lead to the reduction of the level of nuclear armaments and the lessening of tension in the world and the eventual elimination of nuclear armaments . . .

This report gives the bare outline of the disasters which could be associated with the use of nuclear weapons. It discusses the nature and variety of the economic burden they impose. And it unhesitatingly concludes from the considerations that have been set out that whatever the path to national and international security in the future, it is certainly not to be found in the further spread and elaboration of nuclear weapons. The threat of the immeasurable disaster which could befall mankind were nuclear war ever to erupt, whether by miscalculation or by mad intent, is so real that informed people the world over understandably become impatient for measures of disarmament additional to the few measures of arms limitation that have already been agreed to . . . International agreement against the further proliferation of nuclear weapons and agreements on measures of arms control and disarmament will promote the security of all countries. The United Nations has the over-riding responsibility in this field. The more effective it becomes in action, the more powerful its authority, the greater becomes the assurance for man's future. And the longer the world waits, the more nuclear arsenals grow, the greater and more difficult becomes the eventual task.

A dozen years later, the General Assembly, on the initiative of Sweden, requested the Secretary-General to undertake another study on the subject. It was entitled "Comprehensive Study on Nuclear Weapons" and the unanimous report[50] of the experts was submitted in 1980. In his Foreword, the secretary general emphasized that nuclear disarmament continued to be the overriding priority, since nuclear weapons posed the greatest danger to the survival of civilization, and it was necessary to halt and reverse the nuclear arms race in order to avert the danger of a nuclear war. The General Assembly, in resolution 35/156F, expressed its satisfaction with the report that it characterized as a highly significant statement. China voted for the resolution, and France, the Soviet Union, the United Kingdom, and the United States abstained.

The report was truly a comprehensive one. It described and up-dated the great increase in the number of nuclear weapons their rapid technological development, and the awesome and catastrophic destruction and death that would result from their use. It noted that never before had it been possible to carry out destruction on any part of the globe, no matter how distant, and to destroy the very basis for the existence of other states and regions and, perhaps, of mankind itself. It stated that technology often dictates policy instead of serving it and that new systems often emerge not because of any military requirement but because of the sheer momentum of the technological process.

The report also analyzed and criticized the doctrine of nuclear deterrence; it pointed to the risk of a nuclear war being launched by accident due to technical or human error and noted that the majority of international society considered the hazardous concept of a stable balance of terror illusory as a way to permanent security. The report added that "the concept of the maintenance of world peace, stability and balance through the process of deterrence is perhaps the most dangerous collective fallacy that exists."

In their conclusions, the experts recalled Niels Bohr's warning in 1944 that unless agreement to control the new material for nuclear weapons was obtained in due time, these weapons could become a "permanent menace to human society." They also concluded that "nuclear weapons are the most serious threat to international security," and that if political leaders did not accept their responsibility to control technology, "the arms race is certain to go out of control." Finally, they noted that an alternative to the menacing concept of deterrence as a way to maintain peace is to be found in the United Nations, which should be used for all the purposes and stages of disarmament and international security.

The General Assembly, on the initiative of Romania, has also requested the secretary general to undertake three expert studies on the "Economic and Social Consequences of the Arms Race and of Military Expenditures," which have a bearing on the subject of nuclear war.[51]

The first[52] of these reports, in 1971, included the following in its conclusions:

> The acceleration of technological change, the perils which military expenditures have brought in their wake have become so acute that it is no

exaggeration to say that the arms race has finally provided man with the means of putting an end to his species. This is the most obvious of its consequences. Political wisdom has so far averted this final disaster. It cannot, however, insure against military miscalculation or against human or technical error, both of which could lead to the same fearful end . . . The threat of ultimate disaster . . . is by far the most dangerous single peril the world faces today . . . and it far outweights whatever short-term advantage armaments may have achieved in providing peoples with a sense of national security.

The second[53] of these reports, in 1977, contained the following:

The threat of ultimate self-destruction as a result of nuclear war is the greatest peril facing the world. For many years, nuclear arsenals have been sufficient to destroy the entire world, but the accumulation and technological refinement of nuclear weapons continues, enhancing the perils and providing increasingly ample means for the final obliteration of mankind.

Effective security cannot be achieved today by further armament. The world has long since reached the point where security can only be sought in disarmament and in the expansion of international co-operation among all countries in all fields . . .

Nuclear disarmament must be given the highest priority both because of the intolerable threat posed by nuclear weapons, and because current and foreseeable developments in their means of delivery and in the doctrines governing their use, and the prospect of their proliferation to new states will enhance this threat and could make disarmament vastly more difficult in the future . . . Progress in the direction of nuclear disarmament would be greatly facilitated by agreement on certain targets and time-schedules for phased reductions in the nuclear arsenals and for outlawing the use, development, production and possession of these weapons.

The third[54] of these reports, in 1982, considered the problems of the nuclear arms race in somewhat greater depth. The conclusions of the report contained the following:

Driven by an uncontrolled technological momentum and open-ended strategic commitments for attaining a variety of politico-military objectives, the arms race, particularly in the nuclear field, is poised for a new round of escalation in the 1980s . . . The risks of a nuclear war by accident, miscalculation or an act of strategy have increased due to several developments during the period under review. There has also been a reiterated emphasis on enlarging the scope and expanding the reach of strategic doctrines which view the entire world as an integrated multilevel strategic scene.

In a deteriorating international climate, the vicious causation between the technological and strategic aspects of the nuclear arms race, confined essentially to the major military powers, produced a virtual stalemate in the process of nuclear disarmament negotiations. The period under review also underlined the fragility of detente unless it is accompanied by political action in the field of confidence-building and security and meaningful reductions in the massive military build-ups in accordance with the principle of undiminished security as stressed by the Final Document of the Tenth Special Session of the General Assembly (resolution S-10/2). The developments since then represent a step backwards from the international consensus on a disarmament strategy, the immediate goal of which was the elimination of the danger of nuclear war and implementation of measures to halt and reverse the arms race, with a view to achieve general and complete disarmament under effective international control . . .

Since the nuclear arms race constitutes the gravest threat to international security, the nuclear powers owe it as much to themselves as to the rest of the world to take effective measures to first halt and then reverse its course . . . The escalatory spiral of the nuclear arms race cannot be broken without effective measures to stop the testing, stockpiling, production and deployment of nuclear arsenals. If political confidence is a precondition for lowering the levels of military build-ups, then measures of military confidence-building will serve the purpose of both detente and disarmament. For promoting a general lowering of the levels of military build-ups in accordance with the principle of undiminished security, it needs to be remembered that the security of the smallest country is as important for its national well-being as that of the largest military power. International agreements for reducing military build-ups, therefore, require the participation of all countries and a peaceful resolution of all conflict situations . . . Disarmament cannot progress if use of force continues to remain a prevailing factor in present international relations. An international climate should be built in which the existing [conflict] situations would be solved solely by peaceful means and in which refraining from the threat or use of force would become the basic norm of international life. To that end, the mechanisms of the United Nations for the peaceful settlement of disputes should be strengthened and adjusted to present needs, and all states should be encouraged to make full use of them . . .

The vital interest taken by all countries in the cessation of the arms race and in disarmament provides the United Nations with a unique role in organizing a powerful international action for disarmament . . .

The launching of the World Disarmament Campaign by the second special session opens new perspectives for United Nations activities aimed at developing an international conscience and educating world public opinion in favor of disarmament. The present report on the economic and social consequences of the arms race and its extremely harmful effects on world peace and security is the first report to be completed after the conclusion of the second special session and should be considered a contribution to promoting the objectives of the World Disarmament Campaign, namely to inform, to educate and to mobilize world public opinion in favor of disarmament.

All three of the reports on the economic and social consequences of the arms race were unanimously adopted by the experts who prepared them, as were the resolutions[55] of the General Assembly. They welcomed them with satisfaction and requested that they be reproduced and given wide publicity.

Another study undertaken by the Secretary-General with the assistance of experts at the request of the General Assembly was that on a Comprehensive Nuclear Test Ban. The report of that study has been dealt with in the section "A Nuclear Test Ban".[56] Other studies arranged by the Secretary-General are dealt with in the following sections.

It is difficult to evaluate what effect these various studies have had on the work of nuclear disarmament. It is noteworthy that all of them were unanimously agreed to by the respective experts and were the subject of overwhelmingly favorable comment and expressions of appreciation. The Assembly has also directed that they be reproduced and published widely to provide information not only to the United Nations delegations but also to the public. Perhaps a measure of their value is to be found in the fact that there has been a marked increase in the number of such studies requested by the General Assembly.

This assessment would appear to be confirmed by the Final Document of the first Special Session on Disarmament which states: "Taking further steps in the field of disarmament and other measures aimed at promoting international peace and security would be facilitated by carrying out studies by the Secretary-General in this field with appropriate assistance from governmental or consultant experts."

Confidence-Building Measures

The question of confidence-building measures was first given prominence in the United Nations at the 1978 Special Session on Disarmament. The Final Document referred to them in the following terms: "In order to facilitate the process of disarmament, it is necessary to take measures and pursue policies to strengthen international peace and security and to build confidence among states. Commitment to confidence-building measures could significantly contribute to preparing for further progress in disarmament."

In 1979, on the initiative of the Federal Republic of Germany, the General Assembly requested the Secretary-General, by resolution 34/87B, to carry out a comprehensive study on confidence-building measures, with the assistance of governmental experts. Although the study, reported to the General Assembly in 1981,[57] recognized that international confidence could not be created by promoting confidence measures in the military field alone, it paid particular attention to such measures because of their importance.

The study pointed out that, because of the recent deterioration in international relations and the escalation of the arms race, measures to build confidence and facilitate disarmament negotiations had become more urgent. The objective was to reduce or eliminate the causes of mistrust, fear, tensions, and hostilities, all of which contributed to the arms race. The lack of reliable information on the military activities and other matters relating to security and the intentions of states was a principal cause of mistrust. A main objective of confidence-building must be to reduce the elements of fear in order to achieve a more accurate reciprocal assessment of military activities and other matters relating to mutual apprehensions.

Although the experts agreed on the need for exchange of information on the military activities of states and matters relating to mutual security, there were differences concerning the degree of openness required to build confidence. The experts favored regular personal contacts at all political and military levels of decisionmaking in order to achieve a better understanding of reciprocal concerns and to promote cooperation in security-related communication. Such measures were particularly important in times of crisis. But confidence-building measures could not replace measures that would directly limit and reduce military potentials. All organs of the United Nations could contribute to promote agreements on confidence-building measures among governments and they, together with governmental and non-governmental institutions, could help to increase public awareness of the usefulness of such measures for strengthening peace and security and facilitating disarmament measures.

After considering the report, the General Assembly adopted resolution 36/97F, without a vote, which recognized that confidence reflects a set of interrelated factors of a military and non-military character and that a plurality of approaches were needed to overcome fear, apprehension and mistrust between states and to replace them by confidence. It regarded confidence-building measures as a useful approach in reducing and eliminating causes for mistrust, misunderstanding, misinterpretation, and miscalculation; and believed that they would facilitate the process of disarmament. It also invited all states to consider the possible introduction of confidence-building measures in their regions.

In 1982, the General Assembly adopted resolution 37/100D in which it expressed its concern about the deteriorating international situation and the further escalation of the arms race, which reflected and aggravated the unsatisfactory political climate, tension, and mistrust; and it requested the Disarmament Commission to consider elaborating guidelines for appropriate confidence-building measures on a global or regional level. That work is continuing.

An International Space Monitoring System

The idea of creating an international satellite monitoring agency was first proposed by France in 1978 at the Special Session on Disarmament. France noted that surveillance satellites had reached a high level of capability and could play an important role in verifying arms control agreements and in monitoring crises, and it proposed establishing an international satellite monitoring agency (ISMA). The General Assembly, at its regular session later that year, adopted resolution 33/71J, which requested the Secretary-General to appoint a group of governmental experts to study the technical, legal, and financial implications of establishing such an agency.

In 1981, the experts presented their unanimous detailed report[58] that reviewed the state of space technology relating to satellite monitoring and examined the technical requirements and facilities necessary for an ISMA. It also examined the legal implications of the establishment, structure, and functioning of such an agency and provided cost estimates for first setting up a data processing and interpretation center, then establishing ground receiving stations, and finally establishing ISMA's own space surveillance satellites capable of optical, infra-red and radar monitoring. The conclusions of the study were as follows:

The Group recognized the valuable contribution which monitoring by satellites could make to the verification of compliance with certain arms control and disarmament agreements. It further recognized the positive role that satellite monitoring could play in preventing or settling international crises and thus contribute to confidence-building among nations.

From a technical point of view observations from satellites for the purpose of information gathering related to verification of compliance with treaties and for crises monitoring is both possible and feasible. The technical facilities for an International Satellite Monitoring Agency (ISMA), including the satellites necessary to carry out the needed missions, could be acquired in stages: for instance, Phase I could comprise only an image processing and interpretation centre, Phase II could comprise data-receiving stations that could receive appropriate data from observation satellites of various states and in Phase III where the Agency could have its own space segment comprising a number of satellites.

From a legal point of view, there is no provision in international law, including space law, that would entail a prohibition for an international governmental organization such as an ISMA to carry out monitoring activities by satellites.

As regards the financial implications, a variety of technical options are possible, leading to a broad range in cost estimates; a summary of the estimates made by the Group is to be found in the body of the report. Whatever the assumptions on which the estimates are based, even in Phase III, which is the most complete and most expensive phase, an ISMA would cost the international community each year well under 1 per cent of the total annual expenditure on armaments."

In 1982, the General Assembly adopted resolution 37/78K, which stated its conviction that the proposal for the establishment of an ISMA should be pursued in all its aspects, and requested the Secretary-General to report to its 1983 session on the practical modalities for implementing the conclusions of the study with respect to the institutional aspects concerning the membership and organs of an ISMA. China, France and the United Kingdom voted for the resolution, the Soviet Union against, and the United States abstained. The obvious lack of enthusiasm on the part of the two space powers may reflect reluctance to relinquish their present practical monopoly of space surveillance.

It is evident that the establishment of an ISMA is a formidable undertaking that would require some years before becoming operational. However, in view of the very considerable support for the project from the overwhelming majority of the members of the United Nations, and of their hopes concerning its usefulness in economic and other fields in addition to verification, crisis monitoring and peacekeeping, it seems reasonable to look forward to the eventual realization of the idea.

INTERNATIONAL SECURITY

As has been indicated previously, the United Nations has from its earliest years regarded "the problem of security as closely connected with that of disarmament." It said so in those very words in General Assembly resolution 41(1) adopted in 1946 on "Principles governing the general regulation and reduction of armaments." In that resolution, it also recommended that the Security Council accelerate the placing at its disposal of the armed forces mentioned in Article 43 of the Charter.

The Security Council in 1947 established a Commission for Conventional Armaments which in 1948 adopted a set of general principles[58a] which included the following: "A system of regulation and reduction of armaments and armed forces can only be put into effect in an atmosphere of international confidence and security . . ." It added that one of the conditions essential to such confidence and security was "the establishment of an adequate system of agreements under Article 43 of the Charter."

As was explained in the Introduction (chapter 1), it has not been possible up to the present day to implement Article 43 of the Charter; and no armed forces have been made available to the Security Council for enforcing international peace and security, although forces have been made available for specific peacekeeping operations with the consent of the parties to a conflict, and some states have earmarked units of their armed forces for such purposes.

The discussions on international security proceeded along two tracks. The first concerned international security as a problem in itself and dealt with ways of improving it, and the second concerned the relationship between disarmament and international security.

Strengthening International Security

The General Assembly has on many occasions made declarations and recommendations for improving and promoting international peace and security. Among the most noteworthy are two 1970 pronouncements: the "Declaration on the Occasion of the Twenty-Fifth Anniversary of the United Nations" (Resolution 2627 (XXV)), whereby the Members, in solemn and resonant language, reaffirmed their determination to ensure peace and to observe the purposes and principles of the Charter, and the "Declaration on the Strengthening of International Security" (Resolution 2734 (XXV)). In the latter, the Assembly specifically recommended that "the Security Council take steps to facilitate the conclusion of the agreements envisaged in Article 43 of the Charter in order fully to develop its capacity for enforcement action as provided for under Chapter VII of the Charter." The Declaration stressed the close connection between international security, disarmament, and the economic development of countries "so that any progress towards any of these objectives will constitute progress towards all of them." It urged all states, particularly the nuclear powers, to make urgent and concerted efforts for the cessation and reversal of the nuclear and conventional arms race at an early date, the elimination of nuclear weapons, and the conclusion of a treaty on general and complete disarmament. Finally, the Assembly emphasized the need to exert continuous efforts for strengthening international security and requested the Secretary-General to report on the steps taken in pursuance of the Declaration.

Thereafter, the General Assembly has each year discussed the question of implementation of the Declaration on the Strengthening of International Security and has adopted a resolution on it at every session. In recent years, China and the Soviet Union have voted for these resolutions, while France, the United Kingdom, and the United States have abstained.

The resolutions adopted were often similar, repetitive and have become even lengthier, which is understandable since they sought to deal in circumstances of increasing frustration with all the main elements of the problem. Resolution 37/118 adopted in 1982, for example, expressed great concern over the continued escalation of tension in the world; the ever more frequent recourse to the threat or use of force; the continued stalemate in the solution of crises; the continuous escalation of the arms race and military build-up by major powers; the pursuance of policies of rivalry, confrontation and attempts to divide, the world into spheres of influence and domination; the persistence of colonialism, racism, and *apartheid*; the attempts to distort the national liberation struggles; and the lack of solution of the problems of developing countries—all of which endanger international peace and security. The resolution called on all states to refrain from the use or threat of force, intervention, interference, aggression, foreign occupation, and colonial domination or measures of political and economic coercion that violate the sovereignty, territorial integrity, independence, and security of states or their right freely to dispose of their natural resources. It also called on all states, in particular the nuclear weapon states and other militarily significant states, to take immediate steps to promote the Charter system of collective security, together with measures for halting the arms race and for general and complete disarmament. It reiterated its previous call to the Security Council to examine all existing mechanisms in order to enhance the authority and enforcement capacity of the Council and the possibility of holding high-level periodic meetings of the Council so that it could play a more active role in preventing potential conflicts and ensure the implementation of its decisions. The resolution further stated that the promotion of human rights and fundamental freedoms and the strengthening of international peace and security mutually reinforce each other.

In 1982, the General Assembly adopted without a vote resolution 37/119, initiated by Sierra Leone, on "Implementation of the collective security provisions of the Charter for the maintenance of international peace and security." It expressed grave concern over the growing tendency of states to resort to the use of force contrary to the Charter and that the Security Council had not been able to take decisive action, and requested the Secretary-General as a matter of high priority to study the implementation of the collective security provisions of the Charter with a view to strengthening international peace and security.

The fact that the Assembly has found it necessary to repeat year after-year provisions similar to the above is an indication of the difficulties and of its lack of success in strengthening international security.

In the meantime, the Assembly had, in 1977, adopted by consensus resolution 32/155 on a "Declaration on the Deepening and Consolidation of International Detente," which had some similarity to its resolutions on strengthening international security but emphasized especially the importance of detente. The Declaration noted the growing interest in and increased desire for relaxation of tension, and stressed the need to extend this trend to all regions of the world and facilitate the settlement of outstanding international problems by peaceful means. The Declaration also listed confidence-building measures, progress in disarmament, particularly in the nuclear field, the elimination of the threat of war, the establishment of just and equitable economic relations among states, the elimination of all forms of aggression and interference in the internal affairs of other states, strengthening the peace-making and peace-keeping capabilities of the United Nations, and ensuring respect for human rights and fundamental freedoms, as measures that would contribute to the relaxation of tension and to lasting peace. Finally, the Members of the United Nations declared their determination to continue their efforts towards further reduction of tensions and the strengthening of detente by implementing the foregoing list of measures.

The Final Document of the 1978 Special Session on Disarmament also commended the development of detente. It said: "Dynamic development of detente, encompassing all spheres of international relations in all regions of the world, with the participation of all countries, would create conditions conducive to the efforts of states to end the arms race, which has engulfed the world, thus reducing the danger of war. Progress on detente and progress on disarmament mutually complement and strengthen each other."

The Relationship Between Disarmament and International Security

As has been mentioned, the question of the relationship between disarmament and international security had been noted on several occasions by the General Assembly. In the time of the League of Nations, there was a great debate as to whether security or disarmament must come first. From the earliest days of the United Nations, it was recognized that progress must be made in both areas, but the question of priorities and of the amount of progress that might be required in each area and its timing, or the exact correlation between the two were never clarified.

In 1959, the General Assembly unanimously declared in resolution 1378 (XIV) that general and complete disarmament was the most important problem facing the world and called on all Governments to make every effort to achieve a solution of the problem.

In 1961, as a result of direct negotiations between the Soviet Union and the United States (known as the McCloy-Zorin talks), they reached agreement on a Joint Statement of Agreed Principles for Disarmament Negotiations which confirmed the link between disarmament and security. The Joint Statement, which was unanimously accepted by the General Assembly in resolution 1722 (XVI), contained the following:

The United States and the U. S. S. R. have agreed to recommend the following principles as the basis for further multilateral negotiations on disarmament and to call upon other states to co-operate in reaching early agreement on general and complete disarmament in a peaceful world in accordance with these principles:

1. The goal of negotiations is to achieve agreement on a programme which will ensure:
    (a) That disarmament is general and complete and war is no longer an instrument for settling international problems, and
    (b) That such disarmament is accompanied by the establishment of reliable procedures for the peaceful settlement of disputes and effective arrangements for the maintenance of peace in accordance with the principles of the Charter of the United Nations.

. . .

7. Progress in disarmament should be accompanied by measures to strengthen institutions for maintaining peace and the settlement of international disputes by peaceful means. During and after the implementation of the programme of general and complete disarmament, there should be taken in accordance with the principles of the United Nations Charter, the necessary measures to maintain international peace and security, including the obligation of states to place at the disposal of the United Nations agreed manpower necessary for an international peace force to be equipped with agreed types of armaments. Arrangements for the use of this force should ensure that the United Nations can effectively deter or suppress any threat or use of arms in violation of the purposes and principles of the United Nations."

At the Eighteen-Nation Committee on Disarmament, which was convened the following year, the Soviet Union submitted a "Draft treaty on general and complete disarmament under strict international control" on 15 March 1962[59] and the United States an "Outline of basic provisions of a treaty on general and complete disarmament in a peaceful world" on 18 April 1962.[60] Each of the drafts outlined a complete program to be carried out in stages over several years, which integrated measures for disarmament with measures of international security. Because of the wide gulf between the two powers on the approach, the substance, and the timing of the measures, the negotiations soon became deadlocked, and the parties turned to a consideration of partial or collateral measures of disarmament.

While the link between disarmament and international security continued to attract the attention of Members of the United Nations, it was not until they became engaged in preparatory work for the first Special Session on Disarmament that the question became a separate subject for consideration. In 1977, on the initiative of Cyprus, the General Assembly adopted its first resolution (32/87C) on the specific item of the relationship between disarmament and international security. The Assembly considered that a study and determination of the close relationship could promote peace, security, and disarmament, and it requested the Secretary-General to initiate a study and prepare a progress report to the Special Session. The report[61] of the Secretary-General contained a preliminary examination of the relationship between international security and disarmament, of how the linkage had been approached in the United Nations, and of the issues that had risen. It concluded that in view of the fundamental importance of the interrelationship, the subject merited more thorough and systematic consideration.

The 1978 Special Session devoted serious attention to this interrelationship, and the Final Document stated that the secretary general should continue the study. The Final Document also made a number of pronouncements on the subject as follows:

13. Enduring international peace and security cannot be built on the accumulation of weaponry by military alliances nor be sustained by a precarious balance of deterrence or doctrines of strategic superiority. Genuine and lasting peace can only be created through the effective implementation of the security system provided for in the Charter of the United Nations and the speedy and substantial reduction of arms and armed forces, by international agreement and mutual example leading ultimately to general and complete disarmament under effective international control. At the same time, the causes of the arms race and threats to peace must be reduced and to this end effective action should be taken to eliminate tensions and settle disputes by peaceful means.

26. All States Members of the United Nations reaffirm their full commitments to the purposes of the Charter of the United Nations and their obligation strictly to observe its principles as well as other relevant and generally accepted principles of international law relating to the maintenance of international peace and security.

They stress the special importance of refraining from the threat or use of force against the sovereignty, territorial integrity or political independence of any state, or against peoples under colonial or foreign domination seeking to exercise their right to self-determination and to achieve independence; non-intervention and non-interference in the internal affairs of other states; the inviolability of international frontiers; and the peaceful settlement of disputes, having regard to the inherent right of states to individual and collective self-defense in accordance with the Charter.

34. Disarmament, relaxation of international tension, respect for the right to self-determination and national independence, the peaceful settlement of disputes in accordance with the Charter of the United Nations and the strengthening of international peace and security are directly related to each other. Progress in any of these spheres has a beneficial effect on all of them; in turn, failure in one sphere has negative effects on others.

37. Sigificant progress in disarmament, including nuclear disarmament, would be facilitated by parallel measures to strengthen the security of states and to improve in general the international situation.

110. Progress in disarmament should be accompanied by measures to strengthen institutions for maintaining peace and the settlement of international disputes by peaceful means. During and after the implementation of the programme of general and complete disarmament, there should be taken, in accordance with the principles of the United Nations Charter, the necessary measures to maintain international peace and security, including the obligation of states to place at the disposal of the United Nations agreed manpower necessary for an international peace force to be equipped with agreed types of armaments. Arrangements for the use of this force should ensure that the United Nations can effectively deter or suppress any threat or use of arms in violation of the purposes and principles of the United Nations,

At its regular session later in 1978, the General Assembly, by resolution 33/91I, reconfirmed its request that the Secretary-General, with the assistance of experts, continue the study of the relationship between disarmament and international security.

The following year, the General Assembly adopted resolution 34/83A in which it stated that halting the nuclear arms race should be the first step in implementing the Final Document, and it called on all states to eliminate tensions and conflicts and to proceed towards effective collective measures under the Charter for a system of international order, security and peace, concurrently with efforts for disarmament.

In 1980, the Assembly adopted resolution 35/156J, which recommended that early consideration be given to the requirements for halting the arms race, particularly the nuclear arms race, and to developing the modalities for the effective application of the Charter system of international security. It also requested the permanent members of the Security Council to facilitate the work of the Council in carrying out this responsibility.

In 1981, the Secretary-General submitted the expert study[62] on the relationship between disarmaments and international security. The study contains a detailed analysis of the entire question, and the following are its main conclusions:

There are two approaches to enable states to achieve security without reliance on a continuous build-up of armaments . . . One approach is through agreements among states for mutual regulation, limitation and reduction of their armaments and armed forces. The other is to provide security through collective arrangements, such as the system built on the organs and bodies of the United Nations, primarily the Security Council with its responsibility for maintaining international peace and security and its mandate for taking enforcement action if need be.

These approaches are interrelated and they should be pursued in parallel . . . progress in either . . . will greatly facilitate progress in the other; conversely, any set-back in one . . . would be detrimental for the other . . . There can be no fully and effectively operating United Nations Charter system for maintaining international peace and security if the arms race continues unabated and the danger of war continues to rise; nor can there be far-reaching disarmament without the implementation of parallel measures to promote international security . . . The more far-reaching and the more militarily significant the disarmament measures are, the more need there is for co-ordinated measures in the field of strengthening of international security.

To create an effective system of collective security means, in particular, to use the United Nations system more consistently than has been the case in the past. The objective is to increase the confidence of states that the Security Council will involve itself effectively and at an early stage in situations in which international peace and security are threatened; . . . will take the appropriate steps to resolve conflicts as they arise; will see to it that its decisions are implemented; and will avail itself of the means required to enforce its decisions if need be . . . The Group noted . . . that it was important to increase the readiness of the Security Council for prompt and effective action and that that can be achieved, in particular, by the conclusion of the agreements mentioned in Article 43 of the Charter of the United Nations.

The basic requirement of disarmament is that it must preserve or enhance the security of all the states concerned . . . There must be agreements, as appropriate, on means to ensure that the disarmament measures shall be complied with. It is also important that, in the disarmament process, particular attention be paid to reduction of those weapons systems which are particularly destabilizing or which contribute most to over-all insecurity. It is urgent to take steps to halt the arms race, particularly the nuclear arms race, and to take steps to avert nuclear war . . . In particular, measures of disarmament on which negotiations have been initiated could and should be completed and implemented without waiting for the implementation of any further measures of international security.

The United Nations Charter system cannot function effectively without considerable trust, cooperation and unity of purpose in the maintenance of international peace and security among states in general and, above all, among the permanent members of the Security Council . . . To promote the process of disarmament and to ensure the effective functioning of the Security Council, it is particularly important to establish a more permanent cooperative relationship between the Soviet Union and the United States. The promotion of detente and cooperation in general and determined efforts to settle differences and disputes among these States, therefore, assume particular importance . . .

Even in a climate of cooperation and detente, some basic political and other differences among states will remain. It is important to contain these by developing and utilizing more effectively procedures for the peaceful settlement of disputes and by the establishment and faithful respect for principles of international conduct in relations among states. In the long run, only consistent adherence by all states to such principles could provide a solid basis for lasting detente, far-reaching disarmament and sustained international security.

The General Assembly commended the study in resolution 36/97L. It also adopted resolution 36/97K, in which it expressed its view that the best hope for arresting the pernicious spiral of the arms race is by providing means of security for nations other than reliance on the balance of armaments or on deterrence. It called on the Security Council, as a first step towards making its decisions effective, to take the required measures towards implementing Chapter VII of the Charter, which would reinforce the foundations of peace, security, and order and, in so doing, avert the growing threat of nuclear conflagration.

In 1982, the General Assembly again adopted a resolution (37/100E) on disarmament and international security and again requested the Security Council, and particularly its permanent members, to proceed with a sense of urgency to the measures necessary for the effective implementation of its decisions.

In 1982, resolution 37/78B, on international cooperation for disarmament, initiated by Czechoslovakia, had a more urgent note and expressed concern over the danger of a nuclear war; declared that the dissemination of doctrines justifying the unleashing of nuclear war endanger world peace, worsen the international situation and intensify the arms race; called on states to disseminate ideas of international cooperation for disarmament through their educational systems, mass media and cultural policies; and called on UNESCO to consider measures for further mobilizing public opinion for disarmament.

We have witnessed great efforts over the years to strengthen international security and increasing appreciation of the link between and the necessity for parallel progress in both disarmament and international security. In more recent years, there have been suggestions for new approaches towards solving both problems by pursuing detente, greater cooperation between the major powers, and confidence-building measures. There have also been new attempts to press for the implementation of Article 43 of the Charter and to make the Security Council more effective. Far from making significant progress in any of these fields, however, there has been a substantial deterioration in the international situation, a worsening of relations between the two major powers, an escalation in the arms race in both nuclear and conventional weapons, increasing insecurity in the world, and growing fears of the threat of nuclear war.

These developments seem to have led to growing awareness that still greater efforts are necessary in order to avert the threat of nuclear war and, for these efforts to succeed, the requisite political will is necessary.

THE ROLE OF THE PUBLIC

In the last few years, there has been growing recognition by Members of the United Nations of the need to involve the peoples of the world as well as their governments in the efforts for disarmament, and that public opinion could help to generate the necessary political will to achieve agreement.

This recognition was best evidenced at the 1978 Special Session on Disarmament. The Final Document states in paragraph 15:

It is essential that not only Governments but also the peoples of the world recognize and understand the dangers in the present situation. In order that an international conscience may develop and that world public opinion may exercise a positive influence, the United Nations should increase the dissemination of information on the armaments race and disarmament with the full co-operation of Member States.

It also notes in paragraph 10 that "the decisive factor for achieving real measures for disarmament is the 'political will' of states and especially of those possessing nuclear weapons," and paragraph 41 refers to "the political will to reach agreements." For the first time in the long history of disarmament efforts it also lists (in paragraphs 99 to 108 and 123) a number of specific measures in order "to mobilize public opinion on behalf of disarmament."

The measures recommended include the preparation and distribution by governmental and non-governmental information organs of printed and audio-visual material on the dangers of the arms race and on disarmament efforts; the proclaiming of a Disarmament Week each year starting on 24 October to foster the objectives of disarmament; intensification of the activities of the United Nations Centre for Disarmament (since 1 January 1983, the Department for Disarmament Affairs) and of UNESCO to facilitate research and publications on disarmament, and of UNESCO's programme aimed at the development of disarmament education as a distinct field of study; increased participation by non-governmental organizations in disseminating information, and closer liaison between them and the United Nations; the ensuring by member states of a better flow of accurate information on the dangers of the arms race and on disarmament; the development by governments and non-governmental organizations of programs of education for disarmament and peace studies at all levels; the establishment by the United Nations of a program of disarmament fellowships; and increased cooperation by the Centre for Disarmament with non-governmental organizations and research institutes, and also with UN specialized agencies and other institutions to promote studies and information on disarmament.

At its 1978 regular session, the General Assembly adopted, on the initiative of Mongolia, resolution 33/71D on Disarmament Week. The resolution emphasized the urgent need and importance of the mobilization of world public opinion for halting and reversing the arms race, especially the nuclear arms race; it invited governments to undertake activities to promote Disarmament Week, and requested the Secretary-General to report annually to the General Assembly on such activities.

Each year since then, Disarmament Week has been commemorated in a growing number of states and also by the specialized agencies of the United Nations family and by non-governmental organizations. In the context of the World Disarmament Campaign (dealt with later),

Disarmament Week provides an annual focus of a number of activities of the campaign.

In 1978, the General Assembly also adopted, on the initiative of Venezuela, resolution 33/71G on dissemination of information on the arms race and disarmament. The resolution urged Member States, the specialized agencies and the IAEA, as well as non-governmental organizations and concerned research institutes to promote education and information on the arms race and disarmament. It also gave support to the United Nations Disarmament Yearbook and the disarmament periodical published by the Centre for Disarmament and requested the Centre to increase its contacts with non-governmental organizations and research institutions.

As regards education and the dissemination of information about the arms race and disarmament, UNESCO held a World Congress on Disarmament Education in 1980 and has been engaged in a number of follow-up activities, including the preparation of a phased action plan for disarmament education to cover the decade of the 1980s.

The Centre for Disarmament has also been engaged in increasing its contacts with non-governmental organizations, and academic and research institutes, and has stepped up the scope and volume of its publications.

In 1981, on the initiative of Bulgaria, the General Assembly adopted resolution 36/92J, entitled, "World-wide action for collecting signatures in support of measures to prevent nuclear war, to curb the arms race and for disarmament." The resolution considered that the collection of such signatures under the auspices of the United Nations would manifest the will of the world public and would help to create a favorable climate for disarmament, and requested the Secretary-General to prepare a report on the most appropriate form and methods for such world-wide action.

The program of fellowships in disarmament was launched in 1979, with 20 fellows, mainly from developing countries, pursuant to General Assembly resolution 33/71E, and has been continued each year since that time. The second Special Session on Disarmament in 1982 decided to increase the number of fellowships to 25 and later that year the regular session of the General Assembly adopted resolution 37/100G which, *inter alia*, commended the secretary general for the way in which the program had been implemented.

Further developments concerning the role of the public and the mobilization of public opinion are set out in the succeeding section of this study under the heading "World Disarmament Campaign."

Chapter 3

The Current Scene

Negotiations on various measures proposed in the past for a cessation of the nuclear arms races and nuclear disarmament, for banning the use of nuclear weapons, and for reducing the risk of nuclear war are proceeding at the present time. Despite occasional shifts in emphasis and priorities, and setbacks suffered in recent years, the pursuit of nuclear disarmament measures, in particular a comprehensive test ban and a ban on the use of nuclear weapons, continues as a matter of priority.

As the disarmament process continues, new questions emerge or old questions take on a new vitality. Whether old or new, such questions acquire a priority and urgency that bring them to the fore of the international disarmament agenda.

Because of notable developments in the last few years, particularly the increasing concern about such matters as a nuclear weapons freeze, the prevention of nuclear war, and the possible militarization of outer space, I have decided to deal with these matters in a separate chapter of the study under the heading "The Current Scene." This is not intended to imply that only the matters dealt with in this part are current. Indeed, as just mentioned, important efforts to promote a comprehensive nuclear test ban and a ban on the use of nuclear weapons are continuing, as are the crucial negotiations on intermediate-range nuclear forces in Europe and at the strategic arms reduction talks.

The purpose of grouping certain subjects under this heading is to emphasize some of the recent developments that have taken on new importance in the disarmament field.

THE FIRST AND SECOND SPECIAL SESSIONS ON DISARMAMENT

As is apparent from the many references to it throughout this study, the first Special Session on Disarmament in 1978 undertook a survey of all of the problems relating to the arms race and disarmament, and its Final Document is tantamount to a declaration and codification of the current state of disarmament postions at their highest common denominator. The Final Document provided the most comprehensive analysis of the problems of disarmament and peace ever undertaken by the world community and it charted the guidelines for attaining those goals.

The work of the first Special Session and the achievement of consensus on the Final Document was highly praised from all sides. For example, at the close of the Session, the President of the Assembly described the decisions in the Final Document as "very important and, I may say, historic achievements," and the Secretary-General said that at the session there had been "the most extensive and useful discussion of disarmament on a world-wide basis that has yet been held." The United States Representative described the agreement on the Final Document as "a miracle."

The accomplishments of the Special Session were generally viewed as the beginning rather than the end of a process. But the high hopes held were soon disappointed. As the international political situation deteriorated, the hopes for the early implementation of the provisions of the Final Document eroded, and by the time of the second Special Session on Disarmament in 1982, the spirit of optimism had been replaced by a sense of gloom. At the opening of the second Special Session on 7 June 1982, both the President and the Secretary-General, in remarkably similar addresses, drew attention to the following: the failure of the nations of the world to implement the disarmament program that had been adopted by consensus in 1978; the folly of the acceleration of the arms race in the intervening four years and the deterioration of international and national security; the wars raging on several continents; the increasingly dangerous advances in military technology; and the acceptance in some circles of the insane notions that a nuclear war could be "limited" or "winnable." They considered that the current situation was more dangerous and the need for disarmament greater than at the time of the first Special Session and stressed that what was required to arrest and reverse the arms race and avoid the threat of a nuclear holocaust was political will, boldness, and rationality. They were encouraged, however, by the great upsurge of public concern and the activities of non-governmental organizations.

The opening statements of the nuclear powers revealed the wide gap between their positions and indicated the obstacles to making progress.

China was the first nuclear power to speak. It reiterated China's long-standing position that it would never be the first to use nuclear weapons and would under no circumstances use nuclear weapons against non-nuclear states. China called on each of the nuclear states to make similar undertakings. It also announced a new step forward, namely, that "if the two superpowers take the lead in halting the testing, improving or manufacturing of nuclear weapons and in reducing their nuclear weapons by 50 per cent, the Chinese Government is ready to join all other nuclear states in undertaking to stop the development and production of nuclear weapons and to further reduce and ultimately destroy them altogether."

France restated its continued support for its 1979 proposal for creating an International Satellite Monitoring Agency, and expressed regret that the two superpowers, who had a monopoly in this field, had not informed the United Nations of the contribution they would be ready to make. It also linked disarmament to international security and called for increased information and study of the problems of international security and of the balance of forces and arms limitation.

The statement by the Soviet Union attracted much interest. Foreign Minister Andrei Gromyko delivered a message from General Secretary Leonid Brezhnev that dramatically declared: "The Union of Soviet Socialist Republics assumes an obligation not to be the first to use nuclear weapons. This obligation shall become effective immediately." The message called on the other nuclear powers to assume the same obligation, which "would be tantamount in practice to a ban on the use of nuclear weapons althogether." The message also declared, "There is no type of weapons which the Soviet Union would not be prepared to limit or ban on the basis of reciprocity."

In his statement, Gromyko accused the United States of wanting "to scuttle the existing parity" in nuclear arms, and of a "trick" in singling out and wanting to reduce land-based intercontinental ballistic missiles, where the Soviet Union has a numerical advantage, while ignoring the United States advantage in long-range cruise missiles, strategic aircraft, and submarine-launched ballistic missiles, where the

United States "has several times more warheads" than the Soviet Union, as well as the United States' "forward based systems" in Europe and the nuclear capabilities of its NATO allies. He charged that the "unprecedented arms race launched in the United States constitutes the destabilizing factor" and that the United States "militaristic frenzy breeds all sorts of frenzied military doctrines."

President Ronald Reagan, who delivered the United States statement, expressed his "deep concern" over Soviet conduct. He charged that "the decade of so-called detente witnessed the most massive Soviet buildup of military power in history. They increased their defense spending by 40 per cent while American defense spending actually declined in the same real terms. Soviet aggression and support for violence around the world have eroded the confidence needed for arms negotiations." He restated the major proposals of the United States to reduce the risk of war, made at the Intermediate Range Nuclear Force (INF) talks and at the Strategic Arms Reduction Talks (START) in Geneva. In order to improve mutual confidence and reduce the chances of misunderstanding, the United States would propose reciprocal exchanges in such areas as advance notification of major strategic exercises, advance notification of ICBM launchings within and beyond national boundaries, and an expanded exchange of strategic forces data. He also proposed convening an international conference to build on the United Nations work on a common system for reporting military expenditures.

The United Kingdom stressed that nuclear weapons were the deterrents that had kept the peace for thirty-seven years, and there was no better system of preventing war at the present time. It urged that more attention be paid to reducing conventional forces which absorb up to 90 percent of world military budgets. The basic aim of disarmament was to enhance peace and security, and verification was the heart of the disarmament process.

The deep disagreement between the two major nuclear powers prevented the reaching of any consensus agreement on any of the substantive issues before the second Special Session. The only item on which agreement was possible was that dealing with the World Disarmament Campaign, discussed later.

A noteworthy development during the Special Session, however, was the greatly increased role played by the public and by non-governmental organizations and research institutes. The disappointing stalemate and apparent lack of any real sense of urgency inside the U. N. conference halls stood out in sharp contrast to the fervor, sense of commitment, and the impressive mobilization of anti-nuclear public concern outside. A million people rallied in Central Park and in the streets of Manhattan on 12 June (the largest political rally in North American history), and each day there were a number of activities arranged for and by the people who had come from all continents of the earth. Petitions for disarmament signed by 90 million people in nine countries were presented to the Secretary-General. Representatives of 53 international non-governmental organizations and 22 research institutes addressed the delegations, as compared to 25 and 6 respectively at the 1978 session.

Since it was not possible to agree on any substantive Final Document or Declaration, the chairman of the main committee of the whole, Ambassador Oluyemi Adeniji of Nigeria, prepared a set of conclusions for the procedural report,[63] which was approved by the General Assembly. The conclusions stressed the organic relationship between the colossal waste of resources on military programmes and the problems of economic and social development. The prevention of nuclear war was singled out as the most acute and urgent task of the present day. The conclusions also noted the "unanimous and categorical reaffirmation by all Member States of the validity of the Final Document of the first Special Session and their solemn commitment to it and their pledge to respect the priorities in disarmament negotiations as agreed to in its Programme of Action." All Members were urged to consider as soon as possible proposals to secure the avoidance of nuclear war, thus ensuring that the survival of mankind is not endangered.

In his closing address, the president of the Special Session remarked that the lack of success was due to the sad state of the world, where mistrust, conflict, a growing sense of insecurity, and resort to force prevailed. In those conditions, the United Nations could not be expected to function effectively and help create a disarmed and peaceful world. He counted as a positive development the increasing concern of world public opinion, and hoped that the World Disarmament Campaign would raise the level of public conscience. The problem lay in the gap between what people wanted and what their governments were willing to do.

Other speakers noted that the possibilities for agreement were not favorable when relations between the two superpowers were under severe strain with both powers embarking on the greatest arms race in history, each claiming that it must catch up to or keep up with the other. In such circumstances of confrontation, there was little room for compromise or for other powers to play a third party role.

While no agreement on any solution to the substantive problems was achieved, the Special Session did provide a new impetus to the consideration of two problems: a nuclear weapons freeze and the prevention of nuclear war, which were elevated to top positions on the international agenda of disarmament issues.

A NUCLEAR WEAPONS FREEZE

Although the nuclear freeze has received a major new impetus, the concept of freezing nuclear weapons is not a new one. It has been discussed from time to time in one forum or another for a number of years.

In 1964, the United States proposed[64] a verified freeze on the number and characteristics of offensive and defensive strategic nuclear delivery vehicles. The purpose of the proposal was to limit the quantities of strategic nuclear vehicles of the United States and the Soviet Union to their existing levels and to prohibit the development and deployment of new types of such delivery vehicles. The Soviet Union opposed the proposal mainly on the ground that it did not provide for reduction in the number of such delivery vehicles and would preserve the existing American advantage. In 1966, the United States again proposed[65] a freeze on these strategic delivery vehicles, to be followed by reductions in their number. In the same year, the Soviet Union also proposed[66] the destruction of all stockpiles of nuclear weapons and their delivery vehicles and a ban on the production of such weapons and delivery vehicles.

Article VI of the Non-Proliferation Treaty, which was signed on 1 July 1968, appeared to create a legal commitment to seek a nuclear freeze. The parties to the Treaty and, in particular, the Soviet Union, the United Kingdom, and the United States, undertook "to pursue negotiations in good faith on effective measures relating to cessation of the nuclear arms race at an early date and to nuclear disarmament . . ." In the Preamble to the Treaty, they declared "their intention to achieve at the earliest possible date the cessation of the nuclear arms race." "Cessation" means ending or stopping the nuclear arms race, which is tantamount to freezing its qualitative and quantitative levels.

On the same day that the Treaty was signed, the Soviet Union published a Memorandum[67] on Urgent Measures to stop the Arms Race and Achieve Disarmament. Among these measures was an item on "Measures for stopping the manufacture of nuclear weapons and for reducing and destroying stockpiles." It proposed, "in an effort to save mankind from the danger of nuclear war" that "all nuclear powers" immediately begin negotiations on the cessation of production of nuclear weapons, the reduction of stockpiles and the eventual prohibition and elimination of nuclear weapons under appropriate international control.

In 1969, in the introduction[68] to his annual report to the General Assembly, the Secretary-General noted that there existed a rough balance between the Soviet Union and the United States and that this presented a favorable opportunity for freezing that balance and then reducing it to lower and safer levels. He appealed to the two states to begin immediately the bilateral SALT negotiations, and in the meantime to stop all further work on new strategic nuclear weapons either by agreement or by unilateral moratorium by each side.

At the General Assembly that year, on the initiative of Mexico, the Assembly adopted resolution 2602A (XXIV), which appealed to the two nuclear powers to agree, as an urgent preliminary measure in the SALT negotiations, on a moratorium on further testing and deployment of new strategic nuclear-weapon systems. The Soviet Union and the United States were opposed to the resolution, but abstained on the vote.

As was explained earlier in this study, under "Cessation of the Production of Nuclear Weapons and the Reduction and Elimination of their Stockpiles," paragraphs 47 and 50 of the Final Document of the first Special Session called for stopping the qualitative improvement and development of nuclear-weapon systems, and also stopping the production of all types of nuclear weapons and their means of delivery and the production of fissionable material for weapons purposes. These provisions amount to a freeze on all nuclear weapons. (See pp. 55,56).

At the first Special Session, Canada proposed[69] a "strategy of suffocation" of the nuclear arms by arresting it in the laboratories. In a four point proposal, it called for agreement on (1) a comprehensive nuclear test ban, (2) a ban on flight testing new strategic delivery vehicles, (3) cessation of the production of fissionable material, and (4) freezing and then reducing military expenditures on new strategic nuclear-weapon systems. The only initiative taken by Canada to implement the strategy was the series of resolutions it proposed annually from 1978 on the prohibition of production of fissionable material for weapons purposes.[70] At the second Special Session, however, Canada reaffirmed the strategy of suffocation of the nuclear arms race, which it described as a "technological freeze" in the development of new nuclear-weapon systems and proposed that it be "enfolded into a more general policy of stabilization." Canada was the only Western power to deal with the issue of freezing nuclear weapons.

Several neutral and non-aligned countries, however, such as India, Mexico, and Sweden, took the lead in proposing a nuclear weapons freeze at the second Special Session; and they submitted several draft resolutions specifically calling for a freeze on the testing, production, and deployment of all nuclear weapons and their delivery vehicles and for the cessation of the production of fissionaable material for weapons purposes.

Among the nuclear powers, only the Soviet Union dealt with the nuclear freeze. Foreign Minister Gromyko in his main address to the General Assembly stated:

It is likewise very important to securely block all channels for the continuation of the strategic arms race in any form. That means that the development of new types of strategic weapons should be either banned or limited to the extent possible by agreed parameters. We are prepared to agree that the strategic arms of the USSR and the USA be quantitatively frozen already now, the moment the talks begin, and that their modernization be limited to the extent possible.

Although the question of a nuclear freeze became a "hot" issue, because of the opposition of the United States and its allies, there was no possibility of reaching any consensus on it at the second Special Session.

At the 1982 regular session of the General Assembly later in the year, however, the question of a nuclear freeze became a main item of consideration and the Assembly adopted two resolutions on the subject.

In resolution 37/100A, initiated by India, the General Assembly expressed its conviction that nuclear disarmament and the elimination of all weapons of mass destruction had the highest priority in disarmament, and called on all nuclear powers to agree to a freeze on nuclear weapons, which would, among other things, provide for a simultaneous total stoppage of any further production of nuclear weapons and a complete cut-off in the production of fissionable material for weapon purposes.

Resolution 37/100B, initiated by Mexico and Sweden, contains a number of elements that are difficult to summarize and it is therefore quoted in full:

Nuclear arms freeze

The General Assembly,

Recalling that, in the Final Document of the Tenth Special Session of the General Assembly, the first special session devoted to disarmament, in 1978, it expressed deep concern over the threat to the very survival of mankind posed by the existence of nuclear weapons and the continuing arms race,

Recalling also that, on the same occasion, it pointed out that existing arsenals of nuclear weapons were more than sufficient to destroy all life on earth and stressed that mankind was therefore confronted with a choice: halt the arms race and proceed to disarmament, or face annihilation,

Noting that the conditions prevailing today are a source of even more serious concern than those existing in 1978 because of several factors such as the deterioration of the international situation, the increase in the accuracy, speed and destructive power of nuclear weapons, the promotion of illusory doctrines of "limited" or "winnable" nuclear war and the many false alarms which have occurred owing to the malfunctioning of computers,

Believing that it is a matter of the utmost urgency to stop any further increase in the awesome arsenals of the two major nuclear-weapon states, which already have ample retaliatory power and a frightening overkill capacity,

Believing also that it is equally urgent to activate negotiations for the substantial reduction and qualitative limitation of existing nuclear arms,

Considering that a nuclear-arms freeze, while not an end in itself, would constitute the most effective first step for the achievement of the above-mentioned two objectives, since it would provide a favorable environment for the conduct of the reduction negotiations while, at the same time, preventing the continued increase and qualitative improvement of existing nuclear weaponry during the period when the negotiations would take place,

Firmly convinced that at present the conditions are most propitious for such a freeze, since the Union of Soviet Socialist Republics and the United States of America are now equivalent in nuclear military power and it seems evident that there exists between them an over-all rough parity,

1. *Urges* the Union of Soviet Socialist Republics and the United States of America, as the two major nuclear-weapon states, to proclaim, either through simultaneous unilateral declarations or through a joint declaration, an immediate nuclear arms freeze which would be a first step towards the comprehensive programme of disarmament and whose structure and scope would be the following:

(a) It would embrace:

(i)   A comprehensive test ban of nuclear weapons and of their delivery vehicles;

(ii)   The complete cessation of the manufacture of nuclear weapons and of their delivery vehicles;

(iii) A ban on all further deployment of nuclear weapons and of their delivery vehicles;

(iv)   The complete cessation of the production of fissionable material for weapons purposes;

(b) It would be subject to all relevant measures and procedures of verification which have already been agreed by the parties in the case of the SALT I and SALT II treaties, as well as those agreed upon in principal by them during the preparatory trilateral negotiations on the comprehensive test ban held in Geneva.

(c) It would be of a original five-year duration, subject to prolongation in case other nuclear-weapon states join in such a freeze, as the General Assembly expects them to do;

2. *Requests* the above-mentioned two major nuclear-weapon states to submit a report to the General Assembly, prior to the opening of its thirty-eighth session, on the implementation of the present resolution;

3. *Decides* to include in the provisional agenda of its thirty-eighth session an item entitled "Implementation of resolution 37/100B on a nuclear arms freeze."

Both resolutions were adopted by large majorities. The Soviet Union voted for both, France, the U. K. and the U. S. voted against both, and China abstained on the first and did not participate in the vote on the second.

Although the three Western nuclear powers and most of their allies voted against the two resolutions, the concept of freezing the nuclear arms race, as a step towards reducing nuclear weapons, seems to have captured the interest and support of the public, and it can therefore be expected that the question will continue to receive extensive consideration in the future.

PREVENTION OF NUCLEAR WAR

We have seen that the idea of preventing a nuclear war has been a long-standing and recurrent theme of all disarmament efforts. In recent years, interest in it has revived. At the 1981 session of the General Assembly, the questions of preventing the use of nuclear weapons and preventing nuclear war occupied a prominent place in the debates and resulted in the adoption of three resolutions.

Resolution 36/100, entitled "Declaration on the Prevention of Nuclear Catastrophe," initiated by the Soviet Union, proclaimed that the first use of nuclear weapons was a crime against humanity, and that it was the first duty of nuclear states to eliminate the risk of the outbreak of a nuclear conflict. (The question is also dealt with *supra* in chapter 2 under, "No-first-use of Nuclear Weapons." pp. 28, 29).

Resolution 36/92I, entitled "Non-use of Nuclear Weapons and Prevention of Nuclear War," was a continuation of India's efforts to ban the use or threat of use of nuclear weapons and to promote agreement on an international convention on the non-use of nuclear weapons. (See *supra* under chapter 2, "An Absolute Ban on the Use of Nuclear Weapons." pp. 20-26).

The Soviet Union voted for both resolutions, France, the U. K. and the U. S. voted against both, while China did not participate in the vote on the first but voted for the second.

The third resolution, 36/81B, entitled "Prevention of Nuclear War," initiated by Argentina, proposed a new approach. It expressed alarm that the very survival of mankind is threatened by the existence of nuclear weapons and the continuing arms race, recalled that the removal of the threat of a nuclear war is the most acute and urgent task of the present day and that the prevention of nuclear war and reduction of the risks of nuclear war are matters of the highest priority, and called on the nuclear powers to submit to the Secretary-General for consideration at the second Special Session on Disarmament, their views, proposals, and practical suggestions for ensuring the prevention of nuclear war. The resolution was adopted without a vote, which indicates a consensus.

At the second Special Session the subject of prevention of nuclear war was given renewed impetus by the unilateral declaration of the Soviet Union, that became effective immediately, that it would not be the first to use nuclear weapons, and by its call on the other nuclear powers to assume the same obligation.

In the discussions, three proposals[71] were presented on the subject.

The proposal submitted by Bulgaria referred to "the deterioration in the international situation, the growth of nuclear arsenals, the increase in accuracy, speed and destructive power of nuclear weapons, the promotion of dangerous doctrines of 'limited' or 'winnable' nuclear war and the many false alarms which have occurred owing to malfunctioning of computers." It stated that the most effective guarantee against the danger of nuclear war is nuclear disarmament and the complete elimination of nuclear weapons, and proposed, as a first step, that "the use of nuclear weapons and the waging of nuclear war should be outlawed." It welcomed the declarations of no-first-use of nuclear weapons and called on the nuclear-weapon states to show restraint and responsibility and to act in such a way as to eliminte the risk of the outbreak of a nuclear conflict.

The Federal Republic of Germany, Japan, and the Netherlands proposed a text on "Prevention of war, in particular nuclear war" which "could": indicate that conditions today had not improved since 1978 due to factors such as the deterioration of international confidence, the increase of regional conflicts, the growth of both conventional and nuclear arsenals; recall Article 2 of the Charter against the threat or use of force and Article 51 regarding the inherent right of individual or collective self-defense against an armed attack; call on the nuclear-weapon states to maintain their policies to remove the danger of war, in particular nuclear, and of the use of nuclear weapons, and on all states to act in such a manner as to avoid military confrontations and exclude the outbreak of war; refer to existing commitments not to use any weapons, whether conventional or nuclear, except in response to attack; stress the need to harmonize security assurances for non-nuclear weapon states and the importance of inhibiting the further proliferation of nuclear weapons; urge more openness, including on military budgets and military strategy and in particular on nuclear weapons, to enhance confidence and stability; in order to avoid attacks, due to accident, miscalculation, or communications failure, urge improved communication between governments by establishing "hot lines," advance notification of ICBM launches and strategic exercises and by an expanded exchange of strategic forces data; call on nuclear states, in particular the two major ones, to halt and reverse the nuclear arms race by agreement on verifiable reductions in order to establish a stable equilibrium of forces at the lowest possible level.

The proposal submitted by India stressed that if nuclear war broke out, civilization as we know it would cease to exist and there would be a grave threat to the very survival of mankind. Hence any threat or use of nuclear weapons would be a violation of the Charter and a crime against humanity. The danger of nuclear war came from the very existence of nuclear weapons, and the danger had grown with the increase in both the quality and quantity of these weapons and advocacy of doctrines about their possible use. The prevention of nuclear war could be ensured only by stopping all kinds of nuclear weapon proliferation and the complete elimintion of those weapons.*Pending nuclear disarmament, any use or threat of use of nuclear weapons should be banned and a nuclear freeze should be agreed to, and there should be an immediate suspension of all nuclear weapon testing. The General Assembly should appeal to the nuclear-weapon states to initiate urgent action for the prevention of nuclear war. An aroused public opinion against nuclear weapons and for their elimination is the best hope for preventing nuclear war.

Since there was no possibility whatsoever of the Special Session reaching any consensus on the prevention of nuclear war, it was decided that this subject, together with the other items on its agenda, should be taken up at the ensuing regular session of the General Assembly.

At its 1982 regular session, the General Assembly adopted resolution 37/781, initiated by some Third World and non-aligned states, on the Prevention of Nuclear War, which recalled paragraphs 47 to 50 and 56 to 58[72] of the Final Document of the first Special Session dealing with the avoidance of nuclear war, stated that the removal of the threat of a nuclear war is the most acute and urgent task of the present day, and requested the Commitee on Disarmament to undertake, as a matter of the highest priority, negotiations with a view to achieving agreement on appropriate and practical measures for the prevention of nuclear war. China and the Soviet Union voted for the resolution, and France, the U. K. and the U.S. abstained.

The Assembly also adopted resolution 37/78J, initiated by India, on Non-Use of Nuclear Weapons and Prevention of Nuclear War, which expressed alarm over the threat to the survival of mankind posed by the existence of nuclear weapons and the continuing arms race, and reaffirmed that the most effective guarantee against the danger of nuclear war and the use of nuclear weapons is nuclear disarmament and the complete elimination of these weapons. The Assembly considered that the solemn declarations by two nuclear states not to be the first to use nuclear weapons offered an important avenue to decrease the danger of nuclear war, and expressed the hope that the other nuclear-weapon states would consider making similar declarations of not being the first to use nuclear weapons. The Soviet Union voted for the resolution, France, the U. K. and the U. S. voted against, and China abstained.

As in the case of the nuclear freeze, the prevention of nuclear war also appears to have aroused public interest and support and is likely to continue to receive urgent consideration by the United Nations in the future.

THE QUESTION OF ANTI-SATELLITE
AND BALLISTIC MISSLE
DEFENSE SYSTEMS

As was mentioned in chapter 2, the Outer Space Treaty of 1967 banned the orbiting or stationing of nuclear weapons in outer space (see page 58). It did not, however, ban all military activities, which at that time already included the orbiting and stationing of surveillance satellites in outer space.

Since the early 1960s the United States and the Soviet Union each have stationed in outer space a number of satellites that could survey and monitor military activities of each other and of other states. These made it possible for each power to obtain a great deal of useful information about the other's military activities on earth by unilateral or national technical means of observation and surveillance. Both the SALT I and SALT II treaties and other bilateral agreements relied on these satellites as the main "national technical means of verification" to ensure compliance with these agreements. The surveillance satellites facilitated the reaching of agreement on important disarmament measures since they provided available national technical means of verifying compliance with these agreements. The satellites were major factors providing important information to each country about the other's military activities, and this expansion of military information helped to build confidence.

During the 1970s, however, each of the two powers began to undertake research and development of anti-satellite (known as ASAT) systems. Such activities, if they did not involve the use of nuclear weapons, were not prohibited, but they could be very dangerous and destabilizing if they permitted either side to destroy the "electronic eyes, ears and voice" of the other.

Following a United States proposal, the two powers entered into private bilateral talks in June 1978 to discuss the question. In June 1979 these talks were suspended without reaching any agreement.

In the meantime, there was growing concern about the possible militarization of outer space, and the Final Document of the first Special Session stated in this connection: "In order to prevent an arms race in outer space, further measures should be taken and appropriate international negotiations be held in accordance with the spirit of the [Outer Space] Treaty."

In 1981, the Soviet Union proposed that the stationing of weapons of any kind in outer space be prohibited; and it submitted a draft treaty to the General Assembly prohibiting the orbiting or stationing in outer space or on celestial bodies weapons of any kind, and also prohibiting the destruction, damaging, or disturbing of the normal functioning or changing the flight trajectory of space objects of other parties. The Assembly adopted two resolutions on the subject.

The first resolution (36/97C), sponsored by Western states, was entitled "Prevention of an arms race in outer space." It requested the Committee on Disarmament to consider negotiating effective and verifiable agreements to prevent an arms race in outer space and, as a matter of priority, to prohibit anti-satellite systems. China, France, the United Kingdom, and the United States voted for the resolution, and the Soviet Union abstained.

The second resolution (36/99), sponsored by Socialist states, which was entitled "Conclusion of a treaty on the prohibition of the stationing of weapons of any kind in outer space," took into account the Soviet draft treaty and requested the Committee on Disarmament to embark on negotiations to conclude a treaty to prevent the spread of the arms race to outer space. China and the Soviet Union voted for the resolution, and France, the United Kingdom, and the United States abstained.

In 1982, the General Assembly again adopted two resolutions on the subject. The first, sponsored by a number of non-aligned and Socialist states (resolution 37/83), was entitled "Prevention of an arms race in outer space." It favored the resumption of bilateral negotiations between the Soviet Union and the United States, and requested the Committee on Disarmament to establish an *ad hoc* working group to undertake negotiations for agreements to prevent an arms race in outer space in all its aspects. China, France, and the Soviet Union voted for the resolution; the United States cast the only negative vote, and the United Kingdom abstained.

The second resolution (37/99D), sponsored by Western and some non-aligned states, was entitled "Prevention of an arms race in outer space and prohibition of anti-satellite systems." It requested the Committee on Disarmament to continue substantive consideration of negotiating effective and verifiable agreements to prevent an arms race in outer space and, as a matter of priority, an agreement to prohibit anti-satelite systems as an important step toward that objective. It also expressed the hope that the Committee on Disarmament would take the appropriate steps, such as the possible establishment of a working group, to promote those objectives. France, the United Kingdom and the United States voted for the resolution, the Soviet Union abstained, and China did not participate.

It is thus clear that the Members of the United Nations want to prevent an arms race in outer space and also, as a matter of priority, to ban anti-satellite systems.

As was indicated in chapter 2, under "An International Space

Monitoring System," the overwhelming majority of the Members also favor the establishment of an ISMA (see pages 68-70).

It seems clear that they consider that monitoring by satellites can help build confidence and promote disarmament and international security. On the other hand, it is also clear that they would consider an arms race in outer space, and in particular anti-satellite systems, as harmful to these objectives.

In March 1983, President Ronald Reagan, in a national television program, announced that he was directing the undertaking of a long-term research and development program to explore defensive measures against ballistic missiles. He recognized that this formidable technological task might take several decades and stressed that the program would be for research and development at this stage and would be consistent with the ABM Treaty that banned only the deployment of such weapons.

The proposal has not yet been raised or discussed in the United Nations, but it has already led to controversy. Chairman Yuri Andropov immediately described the United States proposal for a ballistic missile defense system as an attempt "to disarm the Soviet Union," which would "open the floodgates to a runaway race of all types of strategic arms, both offensive and defensive." Some disarmament experts in both the United States and in Western European allied countries have expressed fears that the propsal would create more problems and tensions than it would solve and would reopen the debate on ABMs that had been settled more than a decade earlier. Some emphasized that, unless the technology was available simultaneously to both sides, the very possibility that one side might succeed in developing a defense against ballistic missiles could destroy the balance of stability in terms of deterrence and whatever confidence each of the two major powers had that the other could not attack it without suffering unacceptable damage. Thus, it could increase the risks of the outbreak of nuclear war, rather than reduce them.

MORE INFORMATION AND OPENNESS
ABOUT MATTERS RELATING
TO NUCLEAR ARMS

In recent years, there has been increasing frustration over the lack of progress in halting and reversing the arms race, and in particular the nuclear arms race, and growing dissatisfaction with the policies of the two major nuclear powers by the non-nuclear powers, in particular those that are not allied to the Soviet Union or the United States. This has led to a rising demand by such states to be more fully informed about the nuclear arms race and to become more directly involved in the efforts to halt and reverse it. Their aim is to find ways to pressure the two major nuclear powers to stop the madness of their arms race. It seems clear from the increasing number of resolutions they propose— which are almost invariably adopted—and the growing expressions of concern and alarm in these resolutions, that the overwhelming majority of states are almost desperately searching for ways to make their voices heard and to exert greater influence on the two powers in order to keep the arms race from getting out of control and to avert what they perceive to be the growing threat of a nuclear war.

These concerns and efforts have found expression in many ways, such as, for example, the increasing number of expert studies requested of the Secretary-General on various aspects of the arms race and of measures of disarmament.

The Final Document of the first Special Session emphasized in several of its provisions[73] the central role and primary responsibility for disarmament of the United Nations under the Charter. The United Nations should play a more active and strengthened role and should be kept appropriately and duly informed of all steps in this field, whether unilateral, bilateral, regional or multilateral, without prejudice to the negotiations. Since all peoples of the world have a vital interest in the success of disarmament negotiations, all states have a duty to contribute and to participate in disarmament negotiations. To facilitate this, the United Nations should increase the dissemination of information to them on the armaments race and on disarmament, with the full cooperation of Member States.

Following the first Special Session, the General Assembly, on the initiative of France, decided that sustained research and study in the field of disarmament would promote informed participation by all states in the disarmament efforts. It recognized the need of the international community for more diversified and complete data on problems related to international security, the arms race, and disarmament. It accordingly established the United Nations Institute for Disarmament Research.[74]

In 1982, the General Assembly also adopted, on the initiative of Austria, resolution 37/99G on "Measures to provide objective information on military capabilities," which recognized that objective information on the military capabilities, in particular of the nuclear and other militarily significant states, could contribute to building confidence and to the conclusion of disarmament agreements and thus could, help halt and reverse the arms race. It called on all states, in particular the nuclear states and other militarily significant ones, to communicate to the Secretary-General their views and proposals on additional measures to facilitate objective information and objective assessments of military capabilities, and requested the Secretary-General to report on the communications, including an analysis of the possible role of the U. N. in the matter. France, the United Kingdom, and the United States voted for the resolution, the Soviet Union abstained, and China did not participate.

The General Assembly also adopted, on the initiative of Sweden, resolution 37/99J on "Military research and development," which expressed the conviction that increased information on military research and development could promote confidence and enhance the possibility of reaching agreements, and requested the Secretary-General, with the assistance of experts, to carry out a comprehensive study on the scope, role, and direction of the military use of research and development, the mechanisms involved, its role in the overall arms race, in particular the nuclear arms race, and also its impact on disarmament, particularly in relation to major weapons systems, with a view to preventing a qualitative arms race. China, France, and the Soviet Union voted for the resolution and the United Kingdom and the United States abstained.

The establishment of the program of fellowships in disarmament[75] was also based on the idea that an informed public opinion depended on the availability of adequate information and experience in the process of negotiations, and that such a program would increase the number of qualified experts, particularly among the medium-sized and small states and the developing countries.

The concept of and support for an international satellite monitoring agency[76] was also based in part on the idea of more and better information being placed at the disposal of the members of the world community and of their therefore being able to participate more effectively in the work of the United Nations.

Another indication of the desire of the United Nations Members to be more fully informed, and of their hopes to be able to play a greater role in influencing the two major nuclear powers, is to be found in the series of Assembly resolutions, beginning with resolution 2932B (XXVII) in 1972, calling on the Soviet Union and the United States to keep the General Assembly informed in good time on the progress and results of their bilateral SALT negotiations, or to keep it informed in good time of the results of the negotiations. The two nuclear powers at first had a negative attitude on the grounds that the negotiations were complex and were not within the purview of the Assembly. Beginning in 1977, however, the two powers supported the resolutions requesting them to provide "appropriate" information.

In 1982, on the initiative of Mexico, the General Assembly adopted resolution 37/78A, which noted that the Soviet Union and the United States have been conducting two series of bilateral nuclear arms negotiations in Geneva, and requested the two parties to transmit to the Secretary-General not later than 1 September 1983, a joint report or two separate reports on the stage reached in their negotiations for consideration at the 1983 session of the Assembly. It also requested the two parties to bear constantly in mind that not only their national interests but also the vital interests of all the peoples of the world were at stake. The United States cast the only negative vote on the resolution, while the Soviet Union abstained.

In a somewht different category, one that involves exchanges of information and more openness and communication between the nuclear powers and the two European military alliances, are confidence-building measures.[77] There is a growing demand for the two alliances to provide more information such as advance notice of military maneuvres and of missile launchings and more information concerning their strategic forces and military budgets.

The desire for more openness in regard to military matters is exemplified by the efforts of the United Nations to promote a reduction in military budgets as a useful tool, not merely for releasing resources for economic development but also as a means of increasing confidence between states by the exchange of information on military expenditures, thus facilitating disarmament. Because of the difficulties of measuring and comparing different military budgets and deciding what should and should not be included as military expenditures, the General Assembly has, since 1973, authorized a series of expert studies on the technicdal problems involved, and has approved a practical test of a standardized instrument for reporting military expenditures of states. Some Members of the United Nations, including some NATO members, have submitted reports on their military expenditures on the basis of the standardized reporting instrument, but their number is rather small and does not include any countries of the Warsaw Treaty Organization.

In the latest resolution on the subject, initiated by Sweden, in 1982 (37/95B), the Assembly considered that wider participation in the reporting system would promote its further refinement and, by contributing to greater openness in military matters, increase confidence between states, and emphasized that the aim of these activities was to conclude international agreements on the reduction of military expenditures. The Assembly stressed the need for increasing the number of reporting states from different geographic regions and having different budgeting systems, and called on all states to report annually their military expenditures, using the revised reporting instrument. It also requested the Secretary-General, with the assistance of experts, to determine the types of data required and to construct military price indices and purchasing-power parities for the participating states. France, the United Kingdom, and the United States voted for the resolution, the Soviet Union voted against, and China abstained.

Though progress is slow, there appears to be both a growing demand for, and increasing acceptance that, more information, better communication, and more openness would help to promote greater confidence, reduce misunderstandings and mistrust, and facilitate the process of disarmament.

THE WORLD DISARMAMENT CAMPAIGN

As indicated in chapter 2 under, "The Role of the Public," the Final Document of the first Special Session dealt in some detail with the need and modalities for mobilizing world public opinion on behalf of disarmament (pages 79, 80).

It was felt that some coordinated permanent approach would be useful to implement the provisions of the Final Document. In 1980, on the initiative of Mexico, the General Assembly adopted resolution 35/152I on a World Disarmament Campaign, which requested the Secretary-General to carry out an expert study on the organization and financing of the campaign under the auspices of the United Nations.

The Secretary-General's report[79] stated that the general purpose of the Campaign would be to inform, educate, and generate public understanding and support in order to mobilize world public opinion for disarmament. Its conclusions noted that the United Nations system would be the major source of initiative, materials, coordination, and guidance, that the participation of Member States was crucial both in organizing activities and providing support to the efforts of non-governmental organizations, and that the activities of non-governmental organizations, peace research institutes, educational communities, and members of the media would be essential.

At its 1981 session, the General Assembly adopted resolution 36/92C, which commended the study, and requested that the study and opinions on it received from governments be transmitted to the second Special Session on Disarmament for the solemn launching of the Campaign.

The World Disarmament Campaign was launched at the opening meeting of the second Special Session. Several Western states voiced their doubts as to whether the people in all countries would have free access to information about the arms race and disarmament and as to the extent to which they could express their opinions freely and attempt to influence the policies of their governments. Nevertheless, a Working Group reached full agreement on the objectives, the contents, and the modalities of the Campaign.[80] This agreement was approved by the Assembly and was the main achievement of the Session.

The agreed text stated that the campaign is to be carried out "in all regions of the world in a balanced, factual, and objective manner." Further, "The universality of the campaign should be guaranteed by the co-operation and participation of all states and by the widest possible dissemination of information and unimpeded access for all sectors of the public to a broad range of information and opinions . . . Although the means of informing and educating may vary from region to region, the basic thrust . . . should be equally effective in all regions of the world." The United Nations Centre for Disarmament is to provide "the central guidance in coordinating the World Disarmament Campaign within the UN System and in liaison with Governments and NGOs . . . and the substance of the information material to be disseminated . . ." The U. N. Department of Public Information and UNESCO should be given tasks within their fields of competence. The campaign is to "provide an opportunity for discussion and debate in all countries on all points of view relating to disarmament issues."

The Secretary-General was requested to submit to the 1982 regular session of the General Assembly the specifics of the program for the World Disarmament Campaign taking into account the views expressed during the second Special Session, and to submit an annual report on the implementation of the Campaign to subsequent regular sessions of the Assembly. The report[81] of the Secretary-General set out the general framework of the Campaign and stated that it would focus primarily on five major constitutencies—elected representatives, media, non-governmental organizations, educational communities, and research institutes—and would be carried out in cooperation with Member States. The program of activities for 1983 envisaged five areas of activity, namely, United Nations information materials, consisting of publications, including publication of a newsletter on disarmament, and audio-visual materials; interpersonal communication, seminars and training; a number of special events; a publicity program, including support from well-known personalities in the arts, sciences, sports and public affairs; and utilization of United Nations information centers and other field offices.

The 1982 session of the General Assembly adopted three resolutions on the World Disarmament Campaign. Resolution 37/100H, introduced by Bulgaria, invited Member States, in implementing the World Disarmament Campaign, to take into account the proposal on launching a world-wide action for collecting signatures in support of measures to prevent nuclear war, to curb the arms race and for disarmament, and also to cooperate with the United Nations to ensure a better flow of information on the various aspects of disarmament and to avoid disseminating false and tendentious information. The Soviet Union voted for the resolution; France, the United Kingdom and the United States abstained, and China did not participate.

Resolution 37/100I, introduced by Mexico, was adopted without a vote. It approved the general framework and the 1983 program of activities for the Campaign proposed in the Secretary-General's report, invited all Member States to make voluntary contributions to supplement the United Nations resources, decided that a pledging conference for the Campaign should be held at the 1983 session of the General Assembly, and declared that voluntary contributions by non-governmental organizations, foundations, trusts and other private sources would be welcome.

Resolution 37/100J, initiated by the United States, was also adopted without a vote. It recognized that well-informed discussion on all points of view on disarmament issues may have a positive influence on the attainment of progress in disarmament, and expressed the conviction that the best way to build trust and confidence and to advance the conditions which contribute to disarmament is through the cooperation and participation of all states and by the widest dissemination of information and unimpeded access for all sectors of the public to a broad range of information and opinion. It called on Member States to facilitate the flow of a broad range of accurate information on disarmament matters, both governmental and non-governmental, to further the objectives of the World Disarmament Campaign, called on them to encourage their citizens freely and publicly to express their own views on disarmament questions and to organize and meet publicly for that purpose, and requested the Secretary-General to report annually to the General Assembly on implementation of the resolution.

If the World Disarmament Campaign receives adequate funding, and if the United Nations, and in particular the Department for Disarmament Affairs, promotes it with imagination, vigor and commitment, the World Disarmament Campaign cannot only help to inform and educate people but also their governments, and provide a continuing stimulus for cooperation and accountability between them. Thus, it may not only serve to mobilize public opinion but thereby also generate the necessary political will of governments to pursue an early halt and reversal of the arms race. If the objectives, contents and modalities of the Campaign are fully implemented, the decision to launch the World Disarmament Campaign may well prove to be one of the most important decisions taken by the United Nations in the field of disarmament.

Chapter 4

Perspective and Conclusion

The foregoing account of the work and activities of the United Nations to achieve nuclear disarmament and prevent a nuclear war provides ample evidence of the prodigious efforts that have been devoted to that task. Some observers believe that, despite the failure to make any real progress towards achieving a cessation of the nuclear arms race and nuclear disarmament, the fact that there has been no war between major powers nor any global war in the thirty-eight years of the existence of the world organization, which almost inevitably would have led to nuclear war, constitutes a remarkable record of achievement in light of all the difficulties and obstacles. Others regard the record as a sorry spectacle of failure in the light of the exigencies and requirements for human survival.

Few persons would have believed in the early years of the nuclear age, while the nuclear arms race proceeded at an accelerated pace, with each of the two major powers acquiring thousands of thermonuclear warheads, that the failure to eliminate nuclear weapons, or even to establish effective international control over them would not lead soon to a nuclear holocaust.

Some diplomats and scholars, who have been impressed that no nuclear catastrophe has occurred up to the present time, have speculated whether this was due more to good luck than to good management.

Many of these and most of the public, however, seem to be convinced that, unless the nations of the world succeed in bringing the present dangerous situation under control and in halting and reversing the nuclear arms race, we shall probably not be so lucky in the future.

In pondering the causes of the nuclear arms race and why it has proved impossible to stop it, attention has been focused on the failure or inability to implement the collective security provisions of the Charter. Tension, suspicion, mistrust and fear have been much more the hallmarks of relations between states than have confidence, cooperation, or collective security. Concern for national security has undermined the possibilities for establishing international security.

It is noteworthy that the period from 1963 to 1979, when more than a score of treaties and agreements were concluded, was on the whole a period of relaxation of tension, or detente, and of improving relations between the two major nuclear powers. The period was marked by what were considered to be important treaties to curb the nuclear arms race, such as the Partial Test Ban Treaty, the Non-Proliferation Treaty, the SALT I Treaty and Agreements, and the SALT II Treaty. The achievement of a consensus of the nations of the world, great and small, rich and poor, nuclear and non-nuclear, on the Final Document of the first Special Session on Disarmament in 1978, with its agreed program of action for disarmament, was a high-water mark. As has been pointed out in the Introduction, while all the treaties and agreements achieved so far have not served to halt the arms race, or even to slow it down, it was hoped that they were precursors that would lead the way to real disarmament, and in particular nuclear disarmament.

The agreed program of action in the Final Document provided grounds for hoping that the nations of the world were about to embark on the right course to achieve a cessation of the nuclear arms race and nuclear disarmament. They had agreed, *inter alia*, to work for an early comprehensive test ban, rapid progress in the SALT II negotiations, a qualitative and quantitative freeze on nuclear weapons, and on reductions leading to their elimination; also to promote detente, confidence-building measures, and measures for improving international security and economic development. They had also agreed to consider as soon as possible proposals designed to avoid the use of nuclear weapons, and the prevention of nuclear war.

As had been pointed out in the Final Document, and later in the Secretary-General's study on the relationship between disarmament and international security, progress in disarmament and in international security must proceed in parallel, and far-reaching measures of disarmament would not be possible without the implementation of parallel measures to promote international security. Despite the existence of detente, there was no parallel, or indeed any significant progress in implementing the Charter system of collective or international security. In the absence of any real progress in this field, and with technology driving the arms race, that seemed to have acquired an internal dynamic and momentum of its own, with the renewed confrontational rivalry and the resumption of the arms race between the United States and the Soviet Union, it is not surprising that progress in disarmament came to a halt.

What is surprising is the speed with which that occurred. The improvement in the international situation, which had painstakingly been constructed over some two decades, disintegrated in a little over two years. The 1979 SALT II Treaty remained unratified, the second Non-Proliferation Treaty Review Conference in 1980 ended in failure, as did the second Special Session on Disarmament in 1982, the trilateral negotiations for a comprehensive test ban treaty were broken off that same year, and there is renewed talk of ballistic missile defense, which would undermine the ABM Treaty.

The United States maintains that the Soviet Union has obtained superiority over it in nuclear weapons and that it must restore the balance, while the Soviet Union insists that a rough balance in nuclear weapons now exists between the two powers and that the United States is seeking to upset the balance and achieve superiority, which it will not permit.

A measure of the difficulties in bridging the wide gap between the two powers, is to be found in the voting pattern at the 1982 regular session of the General Assembly. As regards the 38 issues on which voting took place related to nuclear disarmament and the prevention of nuclear war, the United States voted in favor of 4 resolutions, against on 20, and abstained on 14; the Soviet Union voted in favor of 30 resolutions, against on 1 and abstained on 7. Of these 38 resolutions, at least 25 had been initiated by non-aligned nations. (In addition to the resolutions that were voted on, 18 other resolutions were adopted without a vote, that is, by apparent consensus.)

There is growing resentment and fear on the part of almost all the non-nuclear states, but in particular of the non-aligned ones, because of the accelerating arms race between the two major powers and the stalemate in disarmament negotiations. The smaller and non-aligned countries are increasingly voicing not only their mistrust of the conduct and actions of the two powers but also suspicion concerning their policies and motivations. They are also beginning to express doubts as to how sincere the two powers really are about disarmament, and question whether the proposals put forward by each of them are not intended more to win some advantage than to gain the acceptance of the other side.

There is also a growing sense and fear that the prospects for preventing the proliferation of nuclear weapons are worsening and the danger of further proliferation are increasing. One of the expected results of the continued vertical proliferation of nuclear weapons by the nuclear powers, in a climate of increasing tension and insecurity, is that it may generate an atmosphere of national insecurity among the nations of the world and a spirit of militarization and national competitiveness that could hasten the horizontal proliferation of these weapons.

The emergence of an additional number of nuclear powers, who might not have a second-strike retaliatory capability, but only an unstable first-strike capacity, would not lead to a situation of wider mutual deterrence or greater stability. To the contrary, it would greatly multiply the risks of nuclear war by accident, miscalculation, desperation, failure of communications, or by deliberate intent. It is the antithesis of the objectives, the efforts and, indeed, the history of the quest for disarmament.

Existing nuclear weapons ready for instantaneous launching can destroy the entire world and, if they spread to additional nations, there is an increasing likelihood that they will do so. And yet the single most effective restraint on the proliferation of these weapons—a comprehensive test ban—is no longer the subject of negotiations.

The present atmosphere in the world is one of foreboding rather than of hope. Some small comfort may be had from the recent development of greater interest in confidence-building measures, which, if pursued, could help restore some confidence and perhaps lead towards a revival of detente.

Some encouragement may also be found in the growing understanding of the need to promote and improve international security if there is to be any hope for far-reaching disarmament. But progress in this field, too, requires a better climate and some degree of mutual confidence and cooperation.

Perhaps more encouraging is the strong support that has developed for a freeze on nuclear weapons. It is a reflection of the fear that science and technology may be getting out of control in the military field, and that reductions in the number of existing weapons are meaningless without a technological or qualitative freeze on the production of new or modernized weapons which, as possible first-strike weapons, are more dangerous and destabilizing.

Another positive development has been the rising consciousness of the growing danger of nuclear war and of the acute and urgent need to prevent that calamity. As the world political and military situation worsens, it becomes even more urgent to take measures for the prevention of a nuclear war.

But effective action on any of these measures is unlikely unless the political will to take such action exists or can be created. All of the questions related to disarmament have been considered at length and their solutions have been suggested in a massive number of resolutions that are repeated annually and, as a result, lose much of their potency. As has been said before, what is needed is not more resolutions, but more resolution. The requisite resolution or political will can be generated only by the pressure of the public on their governments in each country.

Accordingly, the mobilization of public opinion against the arms race and in favor of disarmament and effective measures of international security may be the best and most important way to achieve substantial progress. Indeed, the mobilization of an effective public opinion may be the only way to reverse the mad race to oblivion.

The peoples of the world must convince their governments that the prevention of nuclear war is the most important and urgent problem of our time. Unless a solution can be found for that problem, all other problems may become irrelevant.

The launching of the World Disarmament Campaign would seem to provide an instrument of real hope. Unless the Campaign is utilized successfully, the outlook for humanity is dark indeed. If it is promoted with imagination, skill and dedication, it can become the decisive factor in turning the nations of the world away from the arms race, and towards disarmament and the prevention of nuclear war.

NOTES

1. Resolution 1 (I) adopted on 24 January 1946.
2. *Official Records of the General Assembly*, Sixteenth Session, Annexes, Agenda Item 19, document A/4879.
3. *Official Records of the General Assembly: Tenth Special Session, Supplement No. 4.* Final Document of the Tenth Special Session of the United Nations General Assembly, Resolution S-10/2 of 30 June 1978, paras. 11 and 18.
4. United Nations *Treaty Series*, vol. 472, p. 163.
5. *Ibid.*, vol. 806, p. 402, Legal Registration No. 6839.
6. United Nations *Treaty Series*, vol. 807, p. 57.
7. *Statement of Treaties and International Agreements*, ST/LEG./SER.A/310, p. 13.
8. *Ibid.*, ST/LEG./SER.A/325, p. 30.
9. *Official Records of the General Assembly*, Twenty-Eighth Session, Annexes, agenda item 33., document A/9293.
10. *Arms Control and Disarmament Agreements*, 1982 Edition, United States Arms Control and Disarmament Agency, pp. 275-276.
11. *Official Records of the Atomic Energy Commission*, First Year, No. 1.
12. *Ibid.*, No. 2.

112 / The Prevention of Nuclear War

13. *Official Records of the Disarmament Commission, Supplement for April, May and June 1954*, document DC/SC.1/9 (DC/53, annex 8)
14. *Ibid.*, document DC/SC/1/10 (DC/53, annex 9).
15. *Official Records of the Disarmament Commission, Supplement for April to December 1955*, document DC/SC .1/15/Rev.1 (DC/71, annex 4).
16. *Ibid.*, document DC/SC.1/24 (DC/71, annex 13).
17. *Ibid.*, document DC/SC.1/26/Rev.2 (DC/71/annex 15).
18. *Ibid.*, document DC/SC.1/29/Rev.1 (DC/71/annex 18).
19. *Ibid.*, Supplement for January to December 1957, document DC/SC.1/55
20. *Official Records of the General Assembly, Twelfth Session*, document A/C.1/L.175/Rev.1.
21. *Ibid., First Committee*, 893rd meeting.
22. *Official Records of the Disarmament Commission, Supplement for January 1961 to December 1962*, documents DC/201, 204 and 205.
23. *Official Records of the General Assembly, Thirty-First Session, Annexes*, agenda item 124, document A/31/243, annex.
24. Peiping radio broadcast, October 17, 1964, and *Peking Review*, no. 43, October 23, 1964.
25. *NPT/Conf.* 35/1, annex II, pp. 9-11.
26. *Ibid.*, p. 12.
27. *Ibid.*, annex I, p. 10.
28. *Documents on Disarmament, 1945-1959*, United States Department of State, vol. II, pp. 944-948.
29. Protocol II was signed by the United Kingdom on 20 December 1967, by the United States on 1 April 1968, by France on 18 July 1973, by China on 21 August 1973, and by the Soviet Union on 18 May 1978. All instruments of ratification have also been deposited.
30. China, United Kingdom and United States—*Status of Multilateral Arms Regulation and Disarmament Agreements: Special Supplement to the United Nations Disarmament Yearbook*, vol. 2, 1977, pp. 64-66.
    France—*United Nations and Disarmament 1970-1975*, United Nations Publication No. E.76.IX.1., p. 99.
    Soviet Union—*United Nations Disarmament Yearbook*, vol. 3, 1978, pp. 492-493.
31. See the section "Non-Use of Nuclear Weapons Against Non-Nuclear States," pp. 29-31.
32. *United Nations Publication*, No. E.76.I.7, and document A/10027/Add.1, "Comprehensive Study of the Question of Nuclear-Weapon-Free Zones in All Its Aspects."
33. *Ibid.*, paragraphs 115 and 119.
34. *Official Records of the General Assembly, Twenty-Ninth Session*, Supplement No., 27 (A/9627), Annex II, document CCD/431.
35. *UN document*, A/31/125, annex.
36. *Official Records of the General Assembly, Thirty-fifth Session, Supplement No. 27*, appendix II, vol. II, document CD/130.
37. *Official Records of the General Assembly, Thirty-Fifth Session, Supplement No. 27*, Appendix II (CD, 139), document CD/86, document A/35/257.
38. *Official Records of the General Assembly, Thirty-Sixth Session, First Committee* meeting, 21 October 1981.
39. CD/PV/152.
40. *New York Times*, 20 and 21 July 1982.
41. For the reasons for this unusual procedure, see W. Epstein, *The Last Chance: Nuclear Proliferation and Arms Control*, p. 71-72.
42. See the section "Non-Use of Nuclear Weapons Against Non-Nuclear States", p. 29.

43. NPT/CONF/351.
44. See p. 44 *et seq.* in this book.
45. *United Nations Document A/7601/Add.1.*
46. *United Nations Treaty Series,* vol, 402, No. 5778, p. 72.
47. *Ibid.,* vol. 480, p. 43, Legal Registration No. 8843.
48. *Official Records of the General Assembly, Twenty-Fifth Session,* Supplement No. 28, Legal Registration No. 18678, annex ɩo resolution 2660 (XXV).
49. *United Nations Publication,* E.68.IX.1, Document A/6858.
50. *Ibid.,* No. E.81.I.11, Document A/35/92.
51. All three of these studies were authorized and dealt with under the General Assembly's agenda item "Economic and social consequences of the arms race and its extremely harmful effects on world peace and security."
52. *United Nations Publication,* No. E.72.IX.16, Document A/8469/Rev.1.
53. *Ibid.,* No. E.78.IX.1, Document A/32/88/Rev.1.
54. *United Nations Document* A/37/386.
55. General Assembly resolutions 2831 (XXVI), 32/75 and 37/70.
56. See pp. 43-44 in this book.
57. *United Nations* Document A/36/474.
58. A/AC.206/14.
58. *United Nations Publication, The United Nations and Disarmament 1945-1970,* No. 70 IXI.
59. *Official Records of the Disarmament Commission, Supplement for January to December 1962,* document DC/203, annex 1, section C (ENDC/2).
60. *Ibid.,* section F (ENDC/30).
61. *United Nations Document* A/S-10/7.
62. *United Nations Document* A/36/597.
63. *United Nations Document* A/S-12/32.
64. *Official Records of the Disarmament Commission, Supplement for January to December 1964,* document DC/209, Annex 1, ENDC /120.
65. *Ibid. Supplement for 1966,* document DC/228, annex 1, ENDC/165.
66. *Ibid.* document DC/228, annex 1, ENDC/167.
67. *Ibid. Supplement for 1967 and 1968,* document DC/231.
68. *Official Records of the General Assembly, Twenty-Fourth Session, Supplement No. 1A* (A/7601/Add.1). See also supra, section I.C.3, "The SALT Process."
69. *Official Records of the General Assembly: Tenth Special Session Supplement No. 3,* document A/S-10/AC.1/L.6.
70. See the section, "Other Measures of Nuclear Disarmament", p. 61.
71. *United Nations Document,* A/S-12/32, Annex III.
72. See pages 18, 27-28, 56 in this book.
73. *Official Records of the General Assembly: Tenth Special Session. Supplement No. 4* (A/S-10/4), paragraphs 14, 15, 27, 28 and 114.
74. See resolutions 73/71K, 34/83M and 37/99K IV.
75. See section, "The Role of the Public", p. 79.
76. See section, "An International Space Monitoring System", pp. 68-70.
77. See section, "Confidence-Building Measures", pp. 67-68.
78. *United Nations Publication,* Sales No. E.77.I.6.
79. *United Nations Document,* A/36/458.
80. *United Nations Document,* A/S-12/32, Annex V.
81. *United Nations Document,* A/37/548.

About the Author

William Epstein is a Special Fellow of UNITAR and an occasional consultant on Disarmament to the U. N. Secretary-General and the Canadian Government. He was Director of the Disarmament Division of the U. N. for a number of years. For several years, he was a Senior Research Associate at Carleton University, Ottawa, and has been a Visiting Professor at several Canadian and American Universities. He was a member of the Canadian Delegation to six sessions of the U. N. General Assembly. He was Chairman of the International Group of Experts that prepared the report on Chemical and Biological Weapons (1969), and a member of the Group that prepared the Report on a Comprehensive Test Ban (1980) for the United Nations. He was Technical Consultant to the Commission that prepared the Treaty of Tlatelolco, which created a Nuclear Free Zone in Latin America. He has represented the U. N. Secretary-General at a number of disarmament conferences. He is the Chairman of the Canadian Pugwash Group. He is the author of *The Last Chance; Nuclear Proliferation and Arms Control,* and *We Can Avert a Nuclear War,* and he has published extensively in the field of disarmament and international security.